# Building a Fortress in God
# 13 Lessons on Spiritual Warfare

## Building Foundations: A Spirit-Filled Children's Church Curriculum

### Pastor Tamera Kraft
### Revival Fire 4 Kids Resource

**Mt Zion Ridge Press**
http://mtzionridgepress.com
Managing Editors: Michelle L. Levigne and Tamera Lynn Kraft
Cover Art: Tamera Lynn Kraft

ISBN 13: 978-1-955838-88-7

**Registration and Digital Files (Available for FREE with purchase of the curriculum):** Digital files (jpeg graphics, video clips, other resources) are available to anyone who purchases and registers this curriculum at no additional cost. You can download the resources at a Dropbox link using this QR Code..

Or you can register at this link http://eepurl.com/glsELH or type it in the address box on your browser and fill out the form. We never sell or give away any information we receive.

**DVD:** If you prefer a DVD of JPG images and video clips, email revivalfire4kids@att.net to purchase it for an additional cost.

*Building a Fortress in God* is available in PDF download and print.

All Scripture in this curriculum is from the NIV (2011) Bible unless otherwise designated.

Building Foundations Curriculum is a Revival Fire for Kids resource. For more information about Revival Fire for Kids, check out their website at http://revivalfire4kids.com.

**Materials included:**

13 complete downloadable lessons including 26 object lessons, 26 skits with video, 13 games, 13 Bible Stories, 13 memory verse activities, graphics to be used in PowerPoint slides for 13 lessons, 13 small group discussions or activities, and optional lessons and activities.

Lessons, graphics, videos, and Family Devotion Handouts will be available for immediate download upon registering this curriculum at this link: https://shorturl.at/gpUX8

# How To Use This Curriculum:

**Scriptural Premise:** We have victory and protection in Jesus Christ. He is our fortress.

**Decorations:** Decorations and set design should reflect Army headquarters or have a stone fortress. You can use any image included with this curriculum as a backdrop by projecting the image, using a video projector, onto a box or backdrop and drawing it. We also have a couple of backdrop pics in our downloadable resources. Use your creativity.

You could also buy an Armor of God set online or at your local Christian bookstore for additional props.

**Italics:** Italics are used for Scripture. They are also used in this curriculum for passages or speeches the teacher or worker may want to say in their own words. For skits, italics are only used to designate the person speaking.

**Registration and Digital Files (Available for FREE with purchase of the curriculum):** Digital files (JPG graphics, video clips, other resources) are available to anyone who purchases and registers this curriculum at no additional cost at the QR Code below.

You can also register to receive updates on curriculum, other resources, and news about Revival Fire for Kids. Click on this link http://eepurl.com/glsELH or type it in the address box on your browser and fill out the form to register. We never sell or give away any information we receive.

## Welcome:

*Welcome:* Each lesson will welcome the children with an introduction to that day's message.

*Prayer:* It's important to start each lesson with prayer.

*Rules:* A list of 5 Ups are included in the graphics available after registration. Rehearse the rules every week.

*Theme Song:* Get the kids up and moving at the beginning of every lesson with a fun theme song. Theme song that will work with this curriculum are *Every Victory* by Yancy, *I Am a Christian* by Uncle Charlie, *Armor of God* by Victory of Kids Worship, or *See a Victory* by Elevation.

**Memory Verse:** Every lesson has a memory verse. The verse will be included in a slide and will be illustrated in three ways. You can choose to use any of these illustrations to teach the verse, or you could use all three throughout your lesson.

*Memory Verse Skit:* A puppet or live skit with a Bible puppet is included in each lesson to introduce the Memory Verse. Each puppet skit is also recorded on video in the downloadable resources for churches that don't use puppets.

*Memory Verse Talk:* This is a short talk explaining what the verse means to the children. Memorizing God's Word is important, but it's more important for your students to know what a verse means.

*Memory Verse Activity:* Children learn by seeing, reading, hearing, and doing. The memory verse activity is a simple tool to help students remember the verse.

**Game Time:** A Game Time slide is included with registration for this curriculum. It isn't necessary to include a game with every week's lesson, but if you do, you should have a fun game that relates to the lessons. Game Time is the place for that. You may also want to save the game for last so, if the adult service runs long, you can play games until the parents arrive to retrieve their children.

**Video Clips:** *Building a Fortress in God Countdown* and optional video clips for some lessons are included with the downloadable files. All puppet skits and Sgt. Do Right Skits for each lesson are also available on video in the downloadable resources.

**Offering:** Lessons include a short talk on why children should give in the offering. You can expand the fun by having an offering contest with the boys against the girls. You can use a scale with buckets or have two offering plates and count the money. Once a month or once a quarter, have a special reward for the winning team.

**Praise & Worship:** Each week, a time of praise and worship is included to ready the students' hearts to hear the Word of God. This curriculum does not provide music because every church has different musical needs.

**Lesson of the Week:**

*Skits:* Two skits about each week's lesson are included. One skit uses a Bible puppet to introduce the memory verse for the day. Another skit uses a silly character named Sgt. Do Right. These skits require few props and only two people, the leader and another worker, making them easy for even small churches to use. We also have each skit on video in the downloadable resources for churches who find it difficult to do skits. The video and the script for the skits don't always match exactly.

*Bible Story:* Each week, a Bible story is included to go with the lesson.

*Object Lessons:* At least two object lessons illustrate the points of each week's lesson. Resources for the object lessons are not included.

*Message:* A short message ties up the lesson for the day and asks for a response from the students during altar ministry time.

**Optional Resources:** Optional Resources are included in some lessons with object lessons and other interactive events as suggestions for additional teaching activities. The props for optional resources are not included but are easy to obtain.

**Small Group Chat/Activity:** Some children's ministries prefer to end each children's service with a small group chat, a small group Bible study, or a craft at some time during the week. Small group chat questions, activities, and crafts are included for these purposes. Divide students into small groups of not more than six children. You can divide them by ages or include different ages together. Questions and instructions for activities are included to help the leader facilitate a chat with the students about the lesson. Small group sessions will help your students go home with practical applications for what they have learned.

**Home Application:** Each lesson will include a handout for the children to take home. Each handout will include this week's memory verse, a summary of the lesson, a Bible reading for each day, and a weekly family activity. This handout is available as a printable PDF download in our downloadable resources.

# TABLE OF CONTENTS

*extinguish all the flaming arrows of the evil one.*

Psalm 46:1-2 (NIV) *God is our refuge and strength, an ever-present help in trouble. Therefore we will not fear, though the earth give way and the mountains fall into the heart of the sea,*

Hebrews 4:12 (NIrV) *The word of God is alive and active. It is sharper than any sword that has two edges. It cuts deep enough to separate soul from spirit. It can separate bones from joints. It judges the thoughts and purposes of the heart.*

Ephesians 6:12 (NIV) *For our struggle is not against flesh and blood, but against the rulers, against the authorities, against the powers of this dark world and against the spiritual forces of evil in the heavenly realms.*

Revelation 12:11a (NIV) *They triumphed over him by the blood of the Lamb and by the word of their testimony.*

# Lesson 1 - The Lord is My Light

**Focus Point:** God's Light defeats Darkness.

**Goal:** Students will learn God is stronger than anything in their lives. They can trust Him to protect them.

**Verse of the Day: Psalm 27:1 (NLT)** *The Lord is my light and my salvation, so why should I be afraid. The Lord is my fortress, protecting me from danger, so why should I tremble?*

**Supplies Needed:**

- *Building a Fortress in God* Downloadable Resources
- Kid James Puppet (optional)
- Army uniform costume for skit (optional)
- light switch or flashlight
- posterboard or marker board
- marker
- nightlight
- clear bowl of water
- pepper
- dishwashing liquid
- toothpick
- large clear pitcher or bowl of water
- glass that fits into pitcher or bowl
- 2 large pieces of paper towel

**Opening**: *Building a Fortress in God Countdown* or *Building a Fortress in God* Slide (Available free with registration of this curriculum.)

**Welcome**: (use Building a Fortress in God Lesson 1, slide a) *Welcome to Building a Fortress in God. This is a picture of a fortress. Centuries ago and in Bible times, fortresses were built to protect cities. Because of the high stone walls, the enemy could not get inside to attack. Whenever the enemy was coming, the town's people would run into the fortress where they'd be safe. We have a fortress when Satan, our enemy attacks us. God is our fortress. When we are in God, we are safe. For the next few weeks, we will learn about how we can build a fortress in God.*

**Prayer**: Ask a child to pray over the service.

**Rules**: (use rules slide) Go over the 5 Ups Rules.

Go over the *5 Ups Rules*: 1. Sit up straight. 2. Listen up. 3. Hush up. 4. Don't get up and run around or go to the bathroom. 5. Worship Up! (stand up and participate during praise and worship)

**Theme or Activity Songs:** Choose one or two fast-moving activity or theme songs that go with the curriculum.

**Game Time: Light, No Light** (use game time slide)

*Supplies Needed:* light switch or flashlight.

Play this game like you would a traditional game of Red Light, Green Light. Instead of saying Red Light, Green Light, use the light switch as the cue. Line up the students on one side of the room. When the light is on, they move to the other side of the room as fast as they can. When the light is off, the students must freeze their movements. Anyone who continues to move will have to go to the starting point.

*To win this game, you had to make sure the light was on. To win our spiritual battles, we have to make sure we are walking in the light of the Lord. When we walk in spiritual darkness, fear and worry will be able to attack us.*

**Memory Verse Skit:** (Use Lesson 1, slide b and/or Kid James Skit #1 Video)

*Supplies needed:* Kid James Puppet (optional)

*Kid James:* Howdy, kids. I'm Kid James. I'm a Bible, but not just any Bible. I teach children the Word of God. Today's verse is very important. Psalm 27:1 (NLT) says *The Lord is my light and my salvation, so why should I be afraid. The Lord is my fortress, protecting me from danger, so why should I tremble?*

Everyone gets scared sometimes. It's normal to be afraid of some things. Fear can be a healthy thing. It keeps us from doing dangerous things like walking in the middle of the road or jumping off high places. Fear also happens when bad things happen to us or when we're worried about something bad happening. Everybody is afraid sometimes. The important thing is what we do with that fear. If we run to the Lord, He is our fortress. We don't have to be afraid when we run into our fortress. We just need to call out to Jesus, and He will be our light and salvation. He will protect us when we call out to Him.

## Offering:

*One way we stay in the light of God is to give to Him. God owns everything. When we give ten percent of our allowance or birthday money or any other money we get, we show Him that everything belongs to God. Ten percent means if you receive one dollar, you give ten cents. If you receive ten dollars, you give one dollar in the offering.*

## Skit: Sgt. Do Right Talks About the Armor of Light (optional - use Sgt. Do Right Skit #1 Video)

*Supplies Needed:* Army uniform (optional)

(Sgt. Do Right marches into the room and salutes.)

*Leader:* Excuse me, Sir. Who are you?

*Sgt. Do Right:* Sgt. Do Right reporting as ordered, Sir (Ma'am). My captain told me to report here for training in spiritual warfare.

*Leader:* It's nice to meet you, Sgt. Do Right. We are talking about spiritual warfare. Today we're talking about how God's light protects us.

*Sgt. Do Right:* Then I'm just in time. But how can light protect us? I wear a bulletproof vest in battle, and it acts like armor, so if the enemy shoots my chest, the bullets won't hurt me. Light helps you see, but it can't protect you.

*Leader:* Sergeant, have you ever heard of the armor of light?

*Sgt. Do Right:* The armor of light? I've heard of the armor of God but not the armor of light.

*Leader:* Romans 13:12 says *The night is nearly over; the day is almost here. So let us put aside the deeds of darkness and put on the armor of light.* When we live the way God wants us to and put away sin in our lives, we put on the armor of light. The armor of light will protect us from the darkness that comes against us.

*Sgt. Do Right:* So, Sir (Ma'am), what you're saying is if we live for God, He will be our armor of light.

*Leader:* That's right, Sergeant. God's light is our armor. It protects us from all danger.

*Sgt. Do Right:* What happens when we mess up? What if we do something wrong? Will that make this armor of light that protects us go away?

*Leader:* If you are a Christian and have given your life to God, you don't have to fear. God loves you. All you have to do is ask God to forgive you and help you not to mess up again, and He will. God will be our armor of light as long as we are His.

*Sgt. Do Right:* What if I haven't ever decided to live for God? Will this armor of light still protect me?

*Leader:* That's a different story. Anyone who doesn't belong to God is already walking in darkness. They can't have this armor of light, but the Bible says if we confess our sins and give our lives to Jesus, He will forgive us and make us His children.

*Sgt. Do Right:* I sure wouldn't want to go into battle without any protection. Do you think God would accept me into His army if I asked Him for forgiveness and devoted my life to Him?

*Leader:* Anyone can join God's army at any time. If any of you want to join God's army right now, you can do so. Then you can have this armor of light protecting you from the deeds of darkness.

*Sgt. Do Right:* (closes eyes) Lord, I want to join Your army. Please, forgive me of my sins. I pledge from this point forward my life belongs to You.

*Leader:* Welcome to the Army of God, Sgt. Do Right. You now have your armor of light firmly in place.

(Sgt. Do Right salutes and exits)

## Verse of the Day: **Psalm 27:1 (NLT)** *The Lord is my light and my salvation, so why should I be afraid. The Lord is my fortress, protecting me from danger, so why should I tremble?*

## Memory Verse Talk: Talk to Your Fears (use *Building a Fortress in God* Lesson 1, slide b)

Supplies needed: posterboard or marker board, marker

Ask your students what they are afraid of. You can offer suggestions of things you're afraid of to break the ice. List fears on the posterboard or marker board. Talk about the fears in a way that validates the way each student feels. Talk about how your fears make you feel. *When you are afraid of something, it seems bigger than anything in your life, but it's not.*

Read off each fear and ask your students if the thing they're afraid of is more powerful than God. Tell the students to repeat after you and talk to each fear using today's memory verse. For example, say, *"Bullies, the Lord is my light and my salvation, so why should I be afraid? The Lord is my fortress, protecting me from danger of bullies, so why should I tremble?" Memorizing this verse is important because you can use it against your fears whenever you're afraid. Ask God to be your light and salvation. He is your fortress. He will protect you from danger.*

## Memory Verse Activity: Stand and Recite If

Have the students stand up and recite the memory verse if:

- They ate breakfast today.
- They are wearing blue.
- They brushed their teeth sometime today.
- They went to school this week.
- Other things that apply to your students.
- End with: They love Jesus.

## Bible Story: Elisha and the Army of Angels (Use *Building a Fortress In God*, Lesson 1, slide c)

(2 Kings 6:8-23)

*We talked about fears earlier. Today, I'm going to tell you the story of a man who was afraid. There was a prophet named Elisha who had warned the king of Israel that Aram, a neighboring country, was going to attack. Because of Elisha's warning, the army wasn't where the king of Aram thought it was going to be, so the attack didn't happen. The king of Aram was angry and found out Elisha was the one foiling his plans. God would tell Elisha what the king was planning, and Elisha would warn the Israelites. The king found out where Elisha was living and had his entire army surround Elisha.*

*Elisha was not the man who was afraid. I know you probably thought he was, but Elisha knew God was his light and salvation, so he didn't fear what men could do to him. The man who was afraid was Elisha's servant. He saw the entire Aramean army surrounding two men, him and Elisha. Of course, he was scared. Wouldn't you be? Two against thousands isn't very good odds.*

*Elisha said, "Don't be afraid. The army that fights for us is larger than the army that fights for Aram."*

*At this point, the servant was probably counting themselves, one, two, then the army, one thousand, two thousand. He probably thought Elisha was crazy. Maybe his master had been out in the sun too long.*

*Then Elisha said, "Open his eyes, Lord."*

Show slide c. *The servant looked again and saw an army of angels on chariots with horses surrounding them and blocking the Aramean army from getting to them. He never did have to be afraid. God's army of angels was ready to do whatever it took to protect them.*

*God's army of angels are always near, ready to do whatever it takes to protect us. They probably already have saved us from danger, but we didn't know it because we couldn't see them. God will defend and protect His children from danger.*

**Praise and Worship:** Choose a couple of fast songs and a slow song to lead children into praise and worship. You might want to include a song about the greatness of God or how we don't need to fear. You can have a children's praise team, but until they understand leading praise and worship, have an adult leader or you be the worship leader.

## Object Lessons:

**1. Jesus is Our Light in the Darkness** (Use *Building a Fortress in God* Lesson 1, slide d)

*Supplies needed:* nightlight, bowl of water, pepper, dishwashing liquid, toothpick

*Have you ever been afraid of the dark? I have.* Tell a story about being afraid in a dark place. *When we are in danger or afraid, it feels like we are surrounded by darkness. In a way, we are surrounded by darkness, but Jesus gives us hope.*

Show slide d. *John 8:12 (NIV) says, When Jesus spoke again to the people, he said, "I am the light of the world. Whoever follows me will never walk in darkness, but will have the light of life."*

*When danger or darkness comes against us in our lives, we can turn to Jesus as our light and salvation. Light gets rid of darkness. Another way to say it is light dispels darkness.*

Show nightlight. *When your room is dark at night and you turn on the light, even as small a light as this nightlight, the room is no longer dark.*

*When darkness or danger comes against us, we can trust Jesus to dispel the darkness.*

Pour water into a bowl. *Let's pretend this water is your life.*

*Into everyone's life comes danger or trouble.* Pour the pepper into the bowl of water. Make sure the water is covered in pepper.

*But you know what to do when that happens? Jesus is the light of the world, so you pray and ask Him to dispel the darkness.* Dip the toothpick in dishwashing liquid and stick it in the water. The dishwashing liquid on the toothpick will dispel the pepper.

*Just as this toothpick dispelled the pepper in this water, Jesus will dispel the darkness in your life when you call upon Him.*

## 2. Object Lesson: Jesus is Our Fortress

*Supplies needed:* large clear pitcher or bowl of water, glass that fits into pitcher or bowl, 2 large pieces of paper towel

*We all come across troubles and dangers in life. But if we are God's children, He will be our fortress and protection even when we are in those troubled times.*

Show the paper towel and dip it into the pitcher of water while saying the following.

*This paper towel represents a student who doesn't have Jesus in his life. The water is the troubles and dangers of life. When that student has problems, those problems saturate his life. He has no hope.*

Wad the second paper towel into a ball and place it into the glass. Take the glass and turn it upside down, careful to make sure the paper towel doesn't fall out. This is easier if you use a large piece of paper towel and secure it to the bottom of the glass. Place the glass upside down into the pitcher or bowl of water while you say the following.

*This paper towel represents a child who belongs to God. He still goes through troubles and dangers, but God is his fortress who protects him from danger.*

Take the glass out of the water and show the paper towel isn't wet.

## Message: Jesus Protects Us From Danger

Tell your students a true story about a time you were in danger and God rescued you. If you can't think of a story about your life, tell this true story reported on the news a few years ago. You can find the news report on YouTube at this link. https://youtu.be/8j6eugzZXCM

*This is a true story that was on the news. A boy named Willie Myrick was kidnapped by a stranger. A man threw him in the back seat of a car and took off. Willie prayed, and God told him what to do. He started singing the song **Every Praise is to Our God** and kept singing it when the man yelled at him and told him to stop. Finally, the man stopped the car and pushed Willie out. Then the man took off. The boy was saved by praising God when he was in trouble.*

For response time, pray for God's protection over each student as you anoint him or her with oil.

## Small Group Activity: Building a Fortress

*Supplies needed:* chairs, blankets, flashlights, pillows, boxes to stack.

Explain to your students that you are giving them time to build a fortress using the supplies you're providing. If you want, and there's enough room, you can split them into two fortress building teams that compete against each other.

When they are finished, say this. *These fortresses were fun to build, but they won't really protect us against enemies. That's all right because God is our fortress, and He will protect us from any danger. Sometimes, it doesn't seem like He protected us. Sometimes, we can't see how He protects us, but He's always there. Even if a Christian dies, he is protected because he will live in Heaven with Jesus. Jesus protects him from death and Hell.*

# Lesson 2 - The Name of Jesus

**Focus Point:** The Name of Jesus Christ has power to save, heal, and rescue.

**Goal:** Students will learn that the Name of Jesus Christ is above every name and has power to save, heal, and rescue.

**Verse of the Day: Proverbs 18:10 (NIV)** *The name of the Lord is a fortified tower; the righteous run to it and are safe.*

**Supplies Needed:**

- *Building a Fortress in God* Downloadable Resources
- Kid James Puppet (optional)
- Army uniform costume for skit (optional)
- name badges for everyone
- ball of yarn
- baby book or app
- 18 boxes or blocks
- Scotch tape
- marker
- a lamp or bottle a genie would use or an ornate dish
- flat rocks (one for each student)
- paint
- paint brushes
- permanent marker

**Opening:** *Building a Fortress in God Countdown* or *Building a Fortress in God* Slide (Available free with registration of this curriculum.) Before children's church begins, give every student a name badge to wear. Make sure you also have a name badge.

**Welcome:** *Welcome to Building a Fortress in God. Today we're going to learn about a name that is so mighty and powerful that it is called a Fortress in the Bible. That name is above every name. Can you guess what name it is?* Allow your students to guess. *The name is Jesus Christ, also known as Yahshua the Messiah.*

**Prayer:** Ask a child to pray over the service. Encourage him or her to end the prayer with "In the Name of Jesus. Amen."

**Rules:** (use rules slide) Go over the 5 Ups Rules.

Go over the *5 Ups Rules*: 1. Sit up straight. 2. Listen up. 3. Hush up. 4. Don't get up and run around or go to the bathroom. 5. Worship Up! (stand up and participate during praise and worship)

**Theme or Activity Songs:** Choose one or two fast-moving activity or theme songs that go with the curriculum.

**Game Time: Name Web** (use game time slide)

*Supplies Needed:* ball of yarn

Have children sit or stand in a circle. Join the circle with a ball of yarn. Take the end of the yarn and say, "My name is …" Then throw the yarn to someone in the circle. That student will take hold of the yarn. The student will say "Your name is (the name of the person who threw the yarn) and my name is …" Keep playing the game until everyone has been introduced. You can also keep playing until the yarn makes a large web.

*There is one name that is above every name here. He's the one who holds everything together. That name is Jesus Christ, also known as Yahshua the Messiah.*

**Memory Verse Skit:** (use Lesson 2, slide a and/or Kid James Skit #2 Video)

*Supplies needed:* Kid James Puppet (optional)

*Kid James:* Howdy, kids. I'm Kid James. I'm a Bible, but not just any Bible. I teach children the Word of God. Today's verse is about a name. Proverbs 18:10 (NIV) says *The name of the Lord is a fortified tower; the righteous run to it and are safe.* The name of the Lord is Jesus Christ. He's sometimes called Yahshua the Messiah, I AM, Emmanual, which means God with us, the Son of God, the Son of Man, and the Word of God. All of those names are correct. The importance isn't which name you use for Him. The important thing about using Jesus' name is you, as a Christian who is a child of God, are calling out to your Lord. When we use it that way, it is a name so powerful it can save, heal, and rescue.

## Offering:

*In Proverbs 21:6, Scripture says the righteous give and don't hold back. In other words, if Jesus is Lord of your life, you will want to give in the offering whenever you can. You won't hold back money that the Lord can use to help those in need or to share the Gospel with others.*

**Skit: Sgt. Do Right Talks About the Name of Jesus** (optional - use Sgt. Do Right Skit #2 Video)

*Supplies Needed:* Army uniform (optional)

(Sgt. Do Right marches into the room and salutes.)

*Leader:* Hello, Sgt. Do Right.

*Sgt. Do Right:* Sgt. Do Right reporting as ordered, Sir (Ma'am).

*Leader:* I'm glad you're here. I was briefing these students, ah, cadets about our next weapon for spiritual battle.

*Sgt. Do Right:* Good. My captain says I need more training on how to use weapons. What weapon are we using today?

*Leader:* The Name of Jesus.

*Sgt. Do Right:* You can't attack an enemy with a name. After the enemy catches you, he will laugh at you. That doesn't make any sense.

*Leader:* But we're not talking about any name. The Name of Jesus Christ is powerful because He is Lord. If we have faith in the Name of Jesus Christ, He will act.

*Sgt. Do Right:* Even if He is Lord, Sir (Ma'am), I don't see how His Name is going to do me any good.

*Leader:* Jesus' Name has all the power of Jesus Christ Himself. His name is so powerful, that at the Name of Jesus, everyone will bow down and worship Him. When we call out to Jesus Christ, He will save us, heal us, and rescue us. That's why we always end our prayers by saying, "In the Name of Jesus."

*Sgt. Do Right:* That does sound like a good weapon to have in a battle. If a bully at my boot camp decides to pick on me, I can say, "Go jump in the lake, in Jesus' Name," and he'll have to jump in the lake. I could even tell my captain to give me a promotion to become a general, and if I use Jesus' name, he'll have to do it.

*Leader:* Sgt, that's not the way it works. When you give your life to Jesus, it doesn't mean you can control Him and order Him to do things by saying His Name. He's not a private under you who has to do what you say. When you give your life to Jesus, you're recognizing His control over your life.

*Sgt. Do Right:* So Jesus is like a five-star general?

*Leader:* Higher than that. The Bible calls Jesus the King of Kings and the Lord of Lords.

*Sgt. Do Right:* That's a higher rank than any five-star general on the planet. I get it now. Jesus has all the power. I have to obey His commands.

*Leader:* He does have all the power, and we should obey Him, but Jesus Christ loves us. He uses His Name and His Power to save us, to heal us, and to rescue us from any danger. He cares about us.

*Sgt. Do Right:* That's not like any commanding officer I know, but it's great news. I'll remember to call on His Name when I need help.

(Salutes and exits)

**Verse of the Day: Proverbs 18:10 (NIV)** *The name of the Lord is a fortified tower; the righteous run to it and are safe.*

**Memory Verse Talk: Meaning of Names** (use *Building a Fortress in God* Lesson 2, slide a)

*Supplies needed:* Baby book or baby name app on phone

Ask your students if any of them know what their names mean. Tell them the meaning of your name. If you have time, look up the meaning of each student's name.

*Names are important. Most parents spend a lot of time deciding the right name for their child. Your parents probably looked through baby name books or apps, or they might have named you after someone. Names were even more important in Bible days. Sometimes God would even change somebody's name if the name no longer fit. He did that with the Apostle Peter. Peter was born as Simon. Simon means sand. Jesus changed Simon's name to Peter, which means rock. Peter was a strong rock in the early days of the Christian church.*

*As important as all of your names are, Jesus Christ's name is even more important. Jesus is the English version of the name Yahshua. Yahshua means Son of God. Christ is Jesus' title. It means the Messiah or the Anointed One. His name represents who He is. He is our fortress and our protection. We can call to the Name of Jesus when we need help.*

Have your students repeat the verse a couple of times.

## Memory Verse Activity: Building a Fortress

*Supplies needed:* 18 boxes or 18 blocks, Scotch tape, marker

*Preparation:* Write each word of the verse on a piece of paper and tape it to a separate box or block. To decrease the number of boxes, you can write more than one word on each piece of paper. Make sure to include the verse address.

Divide your students into two teams. Have each team take turns stacking the boxes or blocks to create a wall with the verse on it. Time each team. The team that stacks the boxes or blocks quicker wins.

## Bible Story: Lame Man Healed and People Saved in the Name of Jesus

(Acts 3)

One way to introduce this story to the students is to teach them the classic children's song, ***Walking, and Leaping, and Praising God***. It's a lot of fun if you teach the motions. If you don't know the song, you can learn it from this link on YouTube. https://youtu.be/TnQRNwX92Pw

If you don't want to do the song, you can still have your students do the flowing motions as you tell the story. Rehearse the motions with your students a few times before starting.

- Pray – praying hands
- Money – hold out hand and say, "Give me some."
- Jesus Christ – flex arm muscles and say, "Power."
- Walking – walking motion
- Leaping – jump up and down
- Praising God – hands above head swaying back and forth
- Saved – do walking, leaping, and praising God motions

*At 3:00 in the afternoon, Peter and John went to the temple to pray. Outside the temple gate was a lame man asking for money.*

*Peter said, "Look at us." The lame man did so because he expected them to give him money. "We don't have any money. But we have something even better. The name of Jesus Christ is more powerful than money. It has the power to heal. In the name of Jesus Christ, rise up and walk."*

*Peter took the lame man by the hand and pulled him up. Immediately the man was healed by the power of Jesus Christ. The man was so excited, he went walking, and leaping, and praising God. Only the name of Jesus Christ has the power to heal. He went into the temple with Peter and John still walking, and leaping, and praising God. People saw him and were amazed he was healed.*

*Peter preached and told them how Jesus Christ was raised from the dead, and that only faith in His Name had the power to heal the lame man. He told them to repent and believe on the Name of Jesus Christ. Many of them did.*

*But the leaders of the temple were angry. They didn't want Peter and John to preach in the Name of Jesus. That's still true today. Some people still get angry when you speak the Name of Jesus. But Peter and John didn't back down. They refused to stop preaching and praying in Jesus' name.*

*Peter told them in Acts 4:12 (NIV), "Salvation is found in no one else, for there is no other name under heaven given to mankind by which we must be saved."*

Whether you use the song or tell the Bible story, end by saying this:

*Only the name of Jesus Christ has the power to save, heal, and rescue.*

**Praise and Worship:** Choose a couple of fast songs and a slow song to lead children into praise and worship. You might want to include a song about the name of Jesus. You can have a children's praise team, but until they understand leading praise and worship, have an adult leader or you be the worship leader.

**Object Lessons:**

**1. Praying in Jesus' Name** (Use *Building a Fortress in God* Lesson 2, slides b and c)

*Supplies needed:* a lamp or bottle a genie would use or an ornate dish (optional – use slide b)

*Many people end their prayers with, "In Jesus' Name." It's right to do that because there is power in the Name of Jesus, power to save, power to heal, and power to rescue.*

Show lamp or slide B. *But some people try to use the name of Jesus like a lamp that calls up a genie. Just rub the lamp, ask for what you want, and the genie will give it to you. The Name of Jesus is not a magical name like that to get whatever you want.*

*The power that comes from Jesus Christ's name is the power that comes from calling on and having faith in Jesus Christ Himself. His name is above every name because He is above every person.*

Show slide c. *Philippians 2:9-11 (NIV) says, "Therefore God exalted him to the highest place and gave him the name that is above every name, that at the name of Jesus every knee should bow, in heaven and on earth and under the earth, and every tongue acknowledge that Jesus Christ is Lord, to the glory of God the Father."*

*People will bow down to the name of Jesus because He is Lord, not because the name itself is magical. We pray in the name of Jesus the same way a police officer says, "Stop in the name of the law." The name of the law isn't powerful, but it means the police officer has the power of the law behind him. As Christians, we pray in the name of Jesus Christ because we have faith in the power and authority of Jesus Christ.*

**2. Object Lesson: Jesus' Name is Our Fortified Tower** (Use *Building a Fortress in God*, Lesson 2, slides d - j)

*Supplies needed:* umbrella

Show slide d. *In the Middle Ages, villages built tall stone towers like this one. It would have a ladder out at all times. It would also have enough food and water for a few days. If they had anything valuable, like weapons, they would keep them in the tower. If thieves or murderers started toward the village, the villagers would rush up the ladder into the tower and pull up the ladder. Most thieves didn't carry a ladder around when they planned to rob people. The thieves might get their hands on a few tools or some crops, but the villagers and their valuables would be safe in the tower. Eventually, the bad guys would move on.*

*There are lots of things that keep us safe.* Open the umbrella. *What would this umbrella keep you safe from?* (rain, sun)

Show slide e. *If you were going camping, what would this tent keep you safe from?*

Show slide f. *If a tornado is coming, where would you go to be safe?* (basement, storm shelter, bathtub)

Show slide g. *If an earthquake happened, where would you go to be safe?* (doorway, under heavy table)

Show slide h. *If robbers tried to break into your house, who would you call to rescue you?* (police)

Show slide i. *If your house caught on fire, after you left the house, who would you call to put out the fire?* (firefighter)

Show slide j. *If a stranger tried to snatch you, what would you do?* (Yell "stranger danger")

*There are people and places to run to when you're in danger, or in trouble, or you need help. It is good to know all of these things, but Jesus's name is like the fortified tower the villagers ran into when they were in danger. Whenever you need help or rescue, you can pray and call on the name of Jesus Christ. He will always be there to rescue you.*

## Message: Jesus' Name Saves, Heals, and Rescues

Use *Building a Fortress in God* Lesson 2, slides k - m.

*Jesus Christ's name is more powerful than any other name because He is God. He created everything and has power over everything. No matter what dangers, troubles, or worries you face, the Name of Jesus Christ is more powerful.*

Show slide k. *Only the Name of Jesus has the power to save. There are people out there who say that it doesn't matter who you believe in, but it does because only Jesus has the power to save us from our sins and make us right with God. When we call on the Name of Jesus Christ, He will save us.*

Read Acts 4:12 (NIV). *Salvation is found in no one else, for there is no other name under heaven given to mankind by which we must be saved.*

Show slide l. *The Name of Jesus Christ has the power to heal. Have someone from your church give a testimony about how Jesus healed him or her. Jesus doesn't only heal sicknesses. He can heal depression, ADHD, autism, hurt, fear, worry, or anything else that you need healing from. When we call on the Name of Jesus Christ, He will heal us.*

Read James 5:15 (NIV) *And the prayer offered in faith will make the sick person well; the Lord will raise them up. If they have sinned, they will be forgiven.*

Show slide m. *The Name of Jesus Christ has the power to rescue us. He not only rescues us from physical danger, He rescues us from any trouble we have. When we are in trouble and call on the Name of the Lord, He will be with us through it and keep us safe.*

Read Proverbs:18:10 (NIV) *The name of the Lord is a fortified tower; the righteous run to it and are safe.*

For response time, have students raise their hands if they need to be saved, healed, or rescued.

## Small Group Activity: Worry Rocks

*Supplies needed:* flat rocks (one for each student), paint and brushes, permanent markers

Give each student a rock to paint whatever he wants on it to show worry. When the student is finished, have the student draw a line across the drawing to look like the "no" sign. Tell your students this rock is to remind them they don't have to worry or fear because when they are afraid, they can call on the Name of Jesus and be safe.

While the students are painting their rocks, ask them what worry or fear their rocks represent.

# Lesson 3 - The Holy Spirit Guides Me

**Focus Point:** The Holy Spirit will guide me.

**Goal:** Students will learn that the Holy Spirit will guide them if they listen to Him.

**Verse of the Day: John 16:13a (NIV)** *But when he, the Spirit of truth, comes, he will guide you into all the truth.*

**Supplies Needed:**

- *Building a Fortress in God* Downloadable Resources
- Kid James Puppet (optional)
- Army uniform costume for skit (optional)
- blindfold
- stop sign
- Bible
- rubber ears (optional – point to your own ears)
- traffic light. (optional. Make traffic light with these supplies: cardboard or posterboard, glass, marker, red, yellow, and green tissue paper, scissors, tape or glue, flashlight)
- construction paper in different colors
- scissors
- glue

**Opening:** *Building a Fortress in God Countdown* or *Building a Fortress in God* Slide (Available free with registration of this curriculum.)

**Welcome:** *Welcome to Building a Fortress in God. Today we're going to learn about a helper we Christians have living inside of us. That is the Holy Spirit. If we listen to Him, He will guide us in all of our decisions, so we will know the right thing to do.*

**Prayer:** Ask a child to pray over the service. Encourage him or her to end the prayer with, "In the Name of Jesus. Amen."

**Rules:** (use rules slide) Go over the 5 Ups Rules.

Go over the *5 Ups Rules*: 1. Sit up straight. 2. Listen up. 3. Hush up. 4. Don't get up and run around or go to the bathroom. 5. Worship Up! (stand up and participate during praise and worship)

**Theme or Activity Songs:** Choose one or two fast-moving activity or theme songs that go with the curriculum.

**Game Time: Listen Carefully** (use game time slide)

*Supplies Needed:* blindfold

Choose two students to play the game. One student will be blindfolded, spun, and placed at the back of the room. The other student will stand at the front of the room. The second student will direct the first student to come to him or her using only his or her voice. The catch is all the other students will call out confusing directions at the same time. You can play this game using other students as often as time permits.

Ask the first student these questions. *How easy was it to follow the leader's directions? Were the other voices distracting?*

### Memory Verse Skit: (use *Building a Fortress in God* Lesson 3, slide a and/or Kid James Skit #3 Video)

*Supplies needed:* Kid James Puppet (optional)

*Kid James:* Howdy, kids. I'm Kid James. I'm a Bible, but not just any Bible. I teach children the Word of God. John 16:13a (NIV) says, *"But when he, the Spirit of truth, comes, he will guide you into all the truth."* Sometimes in life, it's hard to know what God wants you to do. You can always trust the Bible for answers, but sometimes, it's difficult to know which Bible verse to listen to. For instance, an unsaved friend invites you to her overnight slumber party. You want to be a good friend to her because you want her to know about Jesus. But she sometimes does things that would violate God's Word – like gossiping about the unpopular girls in school or using bad words. What do you do? We have the Holy Spirit, sometimes called the Spirit of Truth, inside of us. This is a time when you could pray and ask the Holy Spirit to guide you. He knows what the right thing to do is, and He will guide you if you ask Him to and listen carefully.

### Offering:

*1 Corinthians 9:7 (NIV) says "Each of you should give what you have decided in your heart to give…" The Holy Spirit guides us in a lot of different ways. We can even ask Him what we should give in the offering. When you decide in your heart what to give, you should ask the Holy Spirit to help you decide.*

### Skit: Sgt. Do Right Talks About the Inner Witness (optional - use Sgt. Do Right Skit #3 Video)

*Supplies Needed:* Army uniform (optional)

(Sgt. Do Right marches into the room and salutes.)

*Leader:* Hello, Sgt. Do Right.

*Sgt. Do Right:* Sgt. Do Right reporting as ordered, Sir (Ma'am).

*Leader:* I'm glad you're here. We were talking about the inner witness.

*Sgt. Do Right:* What is the inner witness? Are we trying to find someone to testify inside a courtroom? I don't understand.

*Leader:* It's not that kind of witness.

*Sgt. Do Right:* What kind of witness is it, and how will it help me in spiritual warfare?

*Leader:* The Holy Spirit lives on the inside of every Christian. The inner witness is when the Holy Spirit guides us by talking to our spirits.

*Sgt. Do Right:* That's amazing. I sure would like to hear the Holy Spirit talk to me.

*Leader:* You usually can't hear the Holy Spirit with your ears.

*Sgt. Do Right:* Then how will I know when He talks to me? You're not making any sense.

*Leader:* Sometimes the Holy Spirit talks to us through the Word of God, and sometimes He'll use dreams or visions, or He'll have someone give us a message from God. That's called prophecy. But most of the time, the Holy Spirit uses the inner witness.

*Sgt. Do Right:* So what is the inner witness, and how do I get it?

*Leader:* The inner witness is a feeling you get in your spirit. You usually feel it in your stomach. It might be a sense of peace where you know God wants you to do something. Or it might be a sense of danger where you know the Holy Spirit doesn't want you to do something.

*Sgt. Do Right:* Then it's sort of like your conscience.

*Leader:* That's right, but it's a little different. Most people have a conscience telling them something is right or wrong, but only a Christian has the Holy Spirit guiding him. The more we listen to our inner witness, the easier it will be to hear the voice of the Holy Spirit in our spirits.

*Sgt. Do Right:* I sure would like to hear how the Holy Spirit is guiding me. I'll pray and ask Him to help me listen to my inner witness.

(Salutes and exits)

**Verse of the Day: John 16:13a (NIV)** *But when he, the Spirit of truth, comes, he will guide you into all the truth.*

**Memory Verse Talk: Ways the Holy Spirit Guides Us** (use *Building a Fortress in God* Lesson 3, slide a)

Have your students repeat the verse a couple of times.

*The Holy Spirit doesn't only guide us, He guides us into all truth.*

*The first way He does that is by the Bible, God's Word. The Holy Spirit guides us in other ways too. He speaks to our spirits. That's called the inner witness. Sometimes He'll speak through our parents and teachers. He also can guide us through prophecies, dreams, and other ways. We have to do our part. We do that by reading and hearing God's Word and listening for the Holy Spirit to speak to us. We don't normally hear God with our ears. We hear Him in our spirits. We'll learn more about how the Holy Spirit speaks to us later.*

### Memory Verse Activity: Speaking the Word (use *Building a Fortress in God* Lesson 3, slide a)

*Supplies needed:* None

Show slide a. Have the students repeat the verse with you several times. Turn off slide a. Repeat the verse with the students but don't say the last word. If needed, encourage your students to say the last word without you. Repeat, but next time, don't say the last two words. Continue deleting a word until your students can say the verse on their own.

### Bible Story: Paul and the Macedonian Man

Supplies needed: stop sign

(Acts 16:6-10)

Choose 4 students to act out the story with you. Those students will represent Paul, Silas, Timothy, and the Macedonian Man.

*This is a story about some followers of Jesus named Paul* (point to the student representing Paul), *Silas* (point to the second student), *and Timothy* (point to the third student) *who were traveling to share the Gospel with others.*

*They decided to head to Asia.* Have Paul, Silas, and Timothy head toward one corner of the room. Hold up a stop sign and have them stop. *But the Holy Spirit told them to stop.*

*Then they headed another way through Galatia.* Have Paul, Silas, and Timothy head toward another corner of the room. Hold up a stop sign and have them stop. *But the Holy Spirit told them to stop.*

*They weren't sure what to do. Everywhere they went, they were going the wrong way. Finally, they decided to head to Troas.* Have Paul, Silas, and Timothy head toward the third corner of the room. Hold up a stop sign and have them stop. *But the Holy Spirit told them to stop.*

*By this point, the missionaries were very confused.* Have Paul, Silas, and Timothy shrug their shoulders and act confused. *So, they stopped and prayed.* Have disciples pray. *When they didn't hear an answer right away, they decided to make camp and wait. They went to sleep for the night.* Have students lie on the floor and pretend to sleep.

*During the night, Paul had a vision.* Have Paul wake up and the student representing the Macedonian man stand before Paul. *The man said to Paul, "Come over to Macedonia and help us." Paul woke the other disciples and told them what happened.* Have Paul wake the other disciples and tell them what happened. *Then they all started out to Macedonia.*

*This Bible story tells us how we should listen to the leading of the Holy Spirit. The disciples did what they knew to be right, sharing the Gospel with others. When they felt the Holy Spirit tell them they were going the wrong direction, they stopped and went another way. When they were confused about what to do, they stopped, prayed, and waited for direction. Then, when the Holy Spirit showed them what He wanted them to do, they immediately obeyed.*

**Video: Watch Your Step** (Use *Building a Fortress in God* video Lesson 3, **Watch Your Step**)

Play Video.

*If we're not paying attention, we will miss when the Holy Spirit speaks to us.*

**Praise and Worship:** Choose a couple of fast songs and a slow song to lead children into praise and worship. You can have a children's praise team, but until they understand leading praise and worship, have an adult leader or you be the worship leader.

**Object Lessons:**

**1. Object Lesson: The Holy Spirit Uses God's Word to Speak to Us**

*Supplies needed:* Bible, rubber ears or point to your ears

*The Holy Spirit uses a number of ways to speak to us, but He usually doesn't speak in a way we can hear with our ears.* Show ears. *Even most people who have heard the voice of God with their ears have only heard that voice once or twice in their lifetimes.*

*There are other ways the Holy Spirit speaks to us. Sometimes, He'll speak to our spirits. We'll learn about that later. Other times, He'll have somebody give us a word of encouragement or instruction called a prophecy. When that happens, He'll give us peace inside, and we'll know the prophecy is from God. Sometimes we'll see visions. Basically, we'll see pictures or movies in our minds of things that God is showing us. Sometimes, those movies seem so real, we see them better than we see what's around us. That's what happened to the Apostle Paul when he saw the vision of the man from Macedonia. Occasionally, the Holy Spirit will give us a God dream where when we wake up, we'll remember it and know what it means.*

*The Holy Spirit uses all these ways to speak to us at times, but He will always use the Bible, God's Word, to speak to us. Most of the time, we don't have to pray or receive a vision from God to know what to do because the Bible has already told us. For instance, we don't have to have a dream from God to tell us we should obey our parents. God has already told us in*

*His Word. We don't need a vision to be kind to the kid on the playground that nobody talks to and other kids pick on. We know from God's Word how we should love our neighbor as ourselves. What are some other things we know to do or not to do because it's in the Bible?* Allow students to answer.

*The more we read and listen to the Bible, the more we know what the Holy Spirit wants us to do most of the time. Sometimes, the Holy Spirit will show us a Scripture passage in a new way. He will light up the verse, so we have wisdom on what to do in certain situations or we know what God thinks about something. When we read God's word and take it to heart, it's called His Logos Word. But when the Holy Spirit lights up Scripture in this way, it's called a Rhema Word. The more we know the Bible, the more the Holy Spirit will speak to us through it in Logos words and Rhema words.*

If any of your students don't have a Bible, this would be a good time to have Bibles on hand to give away. If any of your students can't read, recommend the YouVersion app where it can be read to them.

**2. Object Lesson: Be Careful Whose Voice You Are Listening To** (Use *Building a Fortress in God* Lesson 3, slides b – f.)

*Supplies needed:* rubber ears or point to your ears

*When we're learning to hear God's voice and obey, we need to be careful not to listen to voices that will lead us in the wrong direction. Here are a few voices we have to be careful not to listen to.*

Show Slide b. *Bad Thoughts: Have you ever had a thought that wasn't your thought? I bet you have, but you didn't know it. When the devil whispers thoughts into our minds, he usually says "I" instead of "you." Sometimes, he might say things like, "I can't do anything right." Sometimes we do have thoughts like that, but sometimes the devil whispers it and we think it's our thought. There are other thoughts that don't please God. Can you name a few?* Have the students answer.

*When we think bad things that don't please God, whether it's our thought or a thought the devil whispered in our ears, we can do two things. We can let those thoughts stay and build a nest.* Show slide c. *Or we can say to that thought, "This doesn't please God. Lord, help me get rid of this thought."*

Show slide d. *Entertainment: Sometimes the things we watch or listen to or the video games we play have bad things we shouldn't listen to.*

Show slide e. *Friends: Do you have friends who always get you in trouble? Some friends always want to convince you to do something wrong. You can invite those friends to church, and you can be friendly with them, but it's not a good idea to spend too much time with a friend who tries to get you to do wrong things.*

Show slide f. *Culture: Culture is a big word that means the world around us. There are a lot of lies people listen to and believe in culture. These lies are demonic. That means the devil has convinced people these lies are true when they go against God. Raise your hands if you've heard some of these lies.*

Lie: *We can't really know the truth about God.*

*The truth is God reveals Himself in His Word and in our spirits.*

Lie: *If you don't like something about yourself like your gender, you can change it.*

*The truth is, God created you to be who you are. If you're a boy, God created you to be a boy. If you're a girl, God created you to be a girl. If you are a certain color or race, it's because God wanted you to be exactly who you are. When you try to be something different, you're going against who God created you to be.*

Lie: *It doesn't matter what we believe.*

*It does matter what we believe because Jesus Christ is the Way, the Truth, and the Life. If we try to get to God by any other way or religion, we won't be saved. Only Jesus can save us. It doesn't matter if you believe in Jesus or not. He still is Lord and the only way of salvation.*

Lie: *That's your truth, but this is my truth.*

*That's not true. There are only truth and lies. Both are not true.*

*Make sure you are listening to the Holy Sprit. Don't let these lies get inside you.*

## Message: The Inner Witness

*Supplies needed:* rubber ears (optional), traffic light. (optional: Make traffic light with these supplies: cardboard or posterboard, glass, marker, red, yellow, and green tissue paper, scissor, tape or glue, flashlight)

*Preparation:* To make a traffic light, cut a rectangle out of cardboard or posterboard. Draw three even circles by using the top of a glass to trace them. Cut red, yellow, and green squares of tissue paper large enough to cover the holes and attach them with tape or glue. Use a flashlight behind tissue paper to light up different colors.)

*Besides the Bible, the way the Holy Spirit will guide us most of the time is by speaking to our spirit.* Show rubber ears or point to your ears. *We don't hear Him with our ears, at least most people don't. We hear Him right here.* Point to your stomach. Show traffic light. *This traffic light will help you know what the Holy Spirit is telling you.*

Light up the red on the traffic light.

*Have you ever done something wrong and felt bad about it? You might have thought, "That was* bad," or "I shouldn't have done that." But you felt it in the pit of your stomach. That was the Holy Spirit telling you it was wrong, that you need to repent. Sometimes, if you go to do something, even something good, and you feel a yucky feeling in your stomach, the Holy Spirit is telling you something is wrong. When that happens you should stop what you're doing.

Once there was a girl around your age named Joan. She prayed God would speak to her spirit. She wanted to go to a party at a friend's house, and her parents gave her permission. But she didn't feel right in the pit of her stomach. She prayed about it, and the feeling got worse, so she didn't go to the party. The next day, she found out that some older kids went to the party and brought alcohol. The parents had to call the police. Because Joan listened to the Holy Spirit, He kept her from danger.

There are other times the Holy Spirit will speak to you with a red light. You might want to watch a TV show or play a video game, and your parents give you permission. It may look like there's nothing wrong with that show or game, but you feel that red light going off in your spirit. You know the Holy Spirit wants you to stop and not play that game. You may not know there's something bad on the third level of the game that neither you nor your parents know about, but the Holy Spirit knows.

When you feel that yucky feeling in your stomach, stop what you're doing and listen to the Holy Spirit speaking to you.

Light up the green light.

Sometimes, when you do something good, you'll get a good feeling in your stomach. You'll feel peace and joy bubble up inside you. That's the Holy Spirit telling you He's pleased with what you are doing. He's giving you a green light. He wants you to keep doing what you're doing. Sometimes, when the Holy Spirit gives you a green light in your spirit, it doesn't make sense. He might want you to lay hands on your friend and pray for her to be healed when you didn't even know she was sick. Or He might want you to tell an adult God hears his prayers and will answer them. It might take a lot of faith to know the light is green when your thoughts are telling you not to do it. One way to know if you are hearing the Holy Spirit correctly is to pray and ask God to make the feeling stronger if it is of Him, but to make the feeling go away if it isn't. If you're still not sure, ask an adult you trust to help you.

Light up the yellow light.

Yellow means caution. Whatever you're doing, slow down. This happens when you are totally confused about what God wants you to do. When this happens, don't do anything. Instead, pray and ask God what He wants you to do. He will give you wisdom. If you still aren't sure, talk to that trusted adult and ask him or her to help you pray and decide.

As you listen for God's voice, it will be easier for you to hear and know what to do.

For response time, anoint and pray for each student to hear and discern God's voice more clearly. Spend some time in worship. After the worship is done, ask your students if any of them heard God speak anything to their spirits.

## Small Group Activity: Traffic Lights

*Supplies needed:* construction paper in different colors, scissors, glue

*Preparation:* Cut red, yellow, and green circles out ahead of time.

Give each student a rectangular sheet of construction paper. Have the students glue red, yellow, and green circles on it to make traffic lights. Talk to the students about how to know if they are getting a green, red, or yellow light in their spirits.

# Lesson 4 - The Joy of the Lord is My Strength

**Focus Point:** The joy of the Lord is my strength.

**Goal:** Students will learn God wants to strengthen them with supernatural joy.

**Verse of the Day: Nehemiah 8:10b (NIV)** *For the joy of the Lord is your strength.*

**Supplies Needed:**

- *Building a Fortress in God* Downloadable Resources
- Kid James Puppet (optional)
- Army uniform costume for skit (optional)
- bean bag
- paper plates
- marker
- 2 sets of 8 happy faces (*Building a Fortress in God* Lesson 4 happy face)
- stop sign
- pitcher full of water
- clear glass
- bowl
- turkey baster
- bottle of Joy dishwashing detergent
- sharp scissors
- clear bowl
- pitcher of water
- whisk

**Opening**: *Building a Fortress in God Countdown* or *Building a Fortress in God* Slide (Available free with registration of this curriculum.)

**Welcome**: *Welcome to Building a Fortress in God. Today we're learning about what gives us strength when things go wrong. The thing that makes us strong is joy.*

**Prayer**: Ask a child to pray over the service. Encourage him or her to end the prayer with "In the Name of Jesus. Amen."

**Rules**: (use rules slide) Go over the 5 Ups Rules.

Go over the *5 Ups Rules*: 1. Sit up straight. 2. Listen up. 3. Hush up. 4. Don't get up and run around or go to the bathroom. 5. Worship Up! (stand up and participate during praise and worship)

**Theme or Activity Songs**: Choose one or two fast-moving activity or theme songs that go with the curriculum.

**Game Time: Choose Joy Bean Bag Toss** (use game time slide)

*Supplies Needed:* bean bag, paper plates, marker

*Preparation:* Use marker to write joy on a few paper plates. Write things like sadness, depression, anger, and other negative emotions on the other plates. You could also make emoji faces representing those emotions. Place the plates on the floor making sure the joy plates are separated by the other plates.

Have the students take turns trying to throw the beanbag so it lands on the joy plates. Give each child three to five chances. At the end of the game, say the following.

*Each day, we have a choice. When bad things happen, we can choose to be upset, or we can pray and ask God to fill us with joy.*

**Memory Verse Skit:** (use *Building a Fortress in God* Lesson 4, slide a and/or Kid James Skit #4 Video)

*Supplies needed:* Kid James Puppet (optional)

*Kid James:* Howdy, kids. I'm Kid James. I'm a Bible, but not just any Bible. I teach children the Word of God. Today's verse is about joy. Nehemiah 8:10b (NIV) says, "For the joy of the Lord is your strength." Sometimes bad things happen in life. When those bad things happen, we don't feel very happy. But joy is different. Things don't have to be going your way for you to be filled with joy. Joy is something that comes from God. He can fill you with joy even when things are bad. That joy gives you strength.

## Offering:

*2 Corinthians 9:7b (NIV) says* "God loves a cheerful giver." *When we give money in the offering, we should be joyful about giving. Today as we receive the offering, let's all clap our hands and cheer.*

**Skit: Sgt. Do Right Talks About Joy** (optional - use Sgt. Do Right Skit #4 Video)

*Supplies Needed:* Army uniform (optional)

(Sgt. Do Right marches into the room and salutes.)

*Leader:* Hello, Sgt. Do Right.

*Sgt. Do Right:* Sgt. Do Right reporting as ordered, Sir (Ma'am). Today, my captain wants me to learn how to be strong in the Lord.

*Leader:* Then you are right on time. We are talking today about what makes us strong in the Lord. Tell me, Sgt. Do Right. Do you ever laugh?

*Sgt. Do Right:* Laugh. I don't understand. I came here to become strong in the Lord. I take that very seriously. It's not the time to laugh.

*Leader:* Our memory verse for today says, "The joy of the Lord is my strength."

*Sgt. Do Right:* That doesn't make sense. How can joy make you strong?

*Leader:* God strengthens us through joy. When He fills us with joy, we can handle anything the world or the devil throws at us. So, if you want to be strong, maybe you should laugh more.

*Sgt. Do Right:* Even if the Bible does talk about joy, it doesn't mean we should laugh or be joyful. We should take spiritual warfare seriously. Joy means, well, it means... It doesn't mean we should be happy, and it certainly doesn't mean we should laugh.

*Leader:* That's not what the Bible says. Philippians 4:4 (NIV) says, "Rejoice in the Lord always. I will say it again: Rejoice!" Rejoice means to delight in.

*Sgt. Do Right:* Okay, I can see that God wants us to delight in Him, but that's different. You're talking about being happy, and laughing, and being filled with joy. Surely God doesn't want that. He wants us to be serious.

*Leader:* Psalm 16:11 says, "You make known to me the path of life; you will fill me with joy in your presence, with eternal pleasures at your right hand."

*Sgt. Do Right:* All right, Ma'am. I'll concede that the Holy Spirit wants to fill us with joy and give us eternal pleasures, but that doesn't mean He wants us to laugh.

*Leader:* Job 8:21 (NIV) says, "He will yet fill your mouth with laughter and your lips with shouts of joy." Laughter and joy make us strong. Laughter makes us healthy, and joy makes it so we can delight in the Lord. So if you want to be strong in the Lord, you should learn to laugh.

*Sgt. Do Right:* (gives a fake laugh)

*Leader:* The Holy Spirit will help you work on that.

*Sgt. Do Right:* Yes, Sir (Ma'am). I'll do my best.

(Salutes and exits)

**Verse of the Day: Nehemiah 8:10b (NIV)** *For the joy of the Lord is your strength.*

**Memory Verse Talk: The Joy of the Lord** (use *Building a Fortress in God* Lesson 4, slide a)

Have your students repeat the verse a couple of times.

*Strength in this verse means a place of safety, protection, refuge, or a fortress. We've been talking a lot over the last few weeks about how Jesus is our fortress. We find our safety and protection in Him. One way He does that is through joy. When we've asked Jesus into our lives and are children of God, He fills us with His joy. Even when bad things happen, we can ask the Holy Spirit who lives inside of us to fill us with His joy. When we do that, He is our strength, our place of safety.*

## Memory Verse Activity: Happy Face Hunt (use *Building a Fortress in God* Lesson 4, slide a)

*Supplies needed:* 2 sets of 8 happy faces (*Building a Fortress in God* Lesson 4 happy face)

*Preparation:* Write each word of the verse and the verse address on the back of each set of happy faces. Hide the happy faces around the room. If there aren't enough places to hide the happy faces, then scatter them throughout the room.

Divide the class into two teams. Instruct the teams to find the happy faces that have each word of the verse on them and sort them in order at the front of the room. Let them know if they find a word that's already been found, leave the happy face where it is for the other team to find. Whichever team finds all the words and places them in order first wins.

## Bible Story: The Disciples Were Filled with Joy

(Acts 13:13-52)

*Paul and Barnabas went to Antioch to preach the Good News that Jesus died on the cross and rose again so that everyone who believes in Him could be saved. Many decided to accept Christ. How do you think Paul and Barnabas felt about that?* Allow students to answer.

*The next week, Paul and Barnabas decided to preach again. The entire city came out to hear them, but the Jewish leaders were jealous. They heckled Paul and Barnabas as they preached and said they weren't telling the truth. How do you think Paul and Barnabas felt then?* Allow students to answer.

*Paul and Barnabas told the Jewish leaders that since they weren't accepting the Gospel, Paul and Barnabas would preach to the people who would listen, the Gentiles. Gentiles are people who aren't Jews. The Word of God spread through the whole region. Now, how do you think Paul and Barnabas felt?* Allow students to answer.

*The Jewish leaders went to other people and told them bad things about Paul and Barnabas that weren't true. Now, all the people the Jewish leaders went to started bullying Paul and Barnabas. They even kicked the disciples out of town. Now, how do you think Paul and Barnabas felt?* Allow students to answer.

*Paul and Barnabas wiped the dust off their feet as they left the town. Then Acts 13:52 (NIV) says, "And the disciples were filled with joy and with the Holy Spirit." All these people came against Paul and Barnabas and kicked them out of town, yet they were filled with joy and with the Holy Spirit.*

*When bad things happen, it doesn't make us feel good. But the Holy Spirit can fill us with joy even when those bad things happen.*

**Praise and Worship:** Choose a couple of fast songs and a slow song to lead children into praise and worship. You can have a children's praise team, but until they understand leading praise and worship, have an adult leader or you be the worship leader.

## Object Lessons:

### 1. Object Lesson: The Holy Spirit Baptizes Us with Joy

*Supplies needed:* pitcher full of water, clear glass, bowl, turkey baster

*How many of you have been baptized in water?* Allow students to answer. *When you are baptized in water, you are completely immersed in water. How many of you have been baptized in the Holy Spirit?* Allow students to answer. *When you're baptized in the Holy Spirit, you are immersed in the Spirit until you begin to speak in tongues. Because you believe in God and love Him, He wants to fill you with His joy. This is called the baptism of joy.*

*1 Peter 1:8 (NIV) says, "Though you have not seen him, you love him; and even though you do not see him now, you believe in him and are filled with an inexpressible and glorious joy."*

*The joy the Holy Spirit fills you with is different than the happiness you get when something good happens to you. When something good happens to you, it makes you happy.* Ask your students about things that make them happy. For each thing they name, use the turkey baster to put a little water in the glass. *Being happy is a good thing, but it is an emotion. It doesn't last. Because anything can take away your happiness, it doesn't help you in times of trouble. It doesn't have strength in it.*

Pour the pitcher of water into the glass until it overflows as you say the following. *The joy of the Lord is different. The Holy Spirit pours joy into you until you overflow. He baptizes you with joy. Every time something bad happens,* pour a little water from the glass into the pitcher, *the Holy Spirit fills you with overflowing joy again.* Pour the pitcher of water into the glass again to overflowing. *There is strength in this joy because the Holy Spirit will flow into you with joy no matter what the circumstances. The Holy Spirit will keep filling you up with joy.* Keep pouring water into the glass.

### 2. Object Lesson: Joy Stealers

*Supplies needed:* bottle of Joy dishwashing detergent, sharp scissors, clear bowl, pitcher of water, whisk

*There are a lot of things in life that try to steal our joy in the Lord.* Name things that might steal joy while you stab the bottle of Joy a number of times. Make sure the Joy dishwashing liquid pours into the bowl.

*If we let these things, they will steal the joy we have in the Lord, but there's something we can do to stop these joy stealers.* Pour water from the pitcher into the bowl. Stir the water and dishwashing liquid vigorously until the bubbles form.

*When we spend time in the presence of God, praying, worshipping, and reading the Bible out loud, nothing can steal our joy. The Holy Spirit will keep filling us with joy and stirring it up until it bubbles up inside us.*

## Video (optional): Filled with Laughter

Find a video on YouTube of a service where people are filled with joy. Here is one you could use. https://www.youtube.com/watch?v=L88V4qAtUDU&t=13s

## Message: Filled with Joy and Laughter

*What happens when you're really happy and joyful to overflowing?* Allow students to answer. *That's right. You laugh. Laughter is a lot of fun, but did you know laughter can heal your sicknesses and make any fear or stress you have go away? Doctors have done studies on it.*

*Laughter will:*

- *Improve your immune system. That means your body will fight off sickness.*

- *Relieve pain. Laughter makes pain go away.*

- *Decreases Stress. Laughter makes it easier to handle stress, anxiety, and fear.*

- *Improve your mood. Laughter makes you feel happier.*

*Scientists have just figured all this out in the last few years, but the Bible told us this many years ago. Proverbs 17:22 (NIV) says, "A cheerful heart is good medicine, but a crushed spirit dries up the bones." God wants us to laugh. When He fills us with joy, He also fills us with laughter.*

*Job 8:21 (NIV) says, "He will yet fill your mouth with laughter and your lips with shouts of joy."*

*Some people believe when God fills you with joy, you should cry, but that's not true. Crying is one way to worship God, but it's not the only way. You can laugh, or run, or jump, or shout.*

*In a few moments, we're going to take some time to praise and worship. I'm going to pray for each of you and ask God to fill you with joy. When that happens, you might feel like laughing. Go ahead and laugh out loud. God wants to fill your mouths with laughter. You might even want to run or jump up and down or show joy in another way. God wants you to express joy when He fills you with joy, so go ahead and express joy. Allow God to baptize you in joy.*

For response time, anoint and pray for each student to be filled with joy. If the Holy Spirit fills you with joy while you're praying for them, don't hold back. Laughter is contagious, especially laughter that comes from the Holy Spirit.

## Small Group Activity: Make Me Laugh

*Supplies needed:* None

Have each student take a turn trying to make the other students laugh. Tell the students to try not to laugh.

## Lesson 5 - My Worship is a Weapon

**Focus Point:** When we worship, God fights our battles.

**Goal:** Students will learn when they are in the presence of God through worship, He will fight their battles for them.

**Verse of the Day: Psalm 91:1-2 (NIV)** *Whoever dwells in the shelter of the Most High will rest in the shadow of the Almighty. I will say of the LORD, "He is my refuge and my fortress, my God, in whom I trust."*

**Supplies Needed:**

- *Building a Fortress in God* Downloadable Resources
- Kid James Puppet (optional)
- Army uniform costume for skit (optional)
- rock
- masking tape
- basketball
- crown (Burger King gives them away free)
- sign that says "scared"
- sign that says "messenger"
- sign the says, "grrr"
- sign that says, "music"
- 2 hats or baseball caps
- armor and swords (optional)
- dishwashing liquid
- clear jar with lid
- clear pitcher of water
- spoon
- red food coloring
- bowl or tray to catch water

**Opening:** *Building a Fortress in God Countdown* or *Building a Fortress in God* Slide (Available free with registration of this curriculum.)

**Welcome:** *Welcome to Building a Fortress in God. One of the most important ways to fight spiritual warfare is to worship God. When we worship God, we are allowing Him to fight our battles for us.*

**Prayer:** Ask a child to pray over the service. Encourage him or her to end the prayer with "In the Name of Jesus. Amen."

**Rules:** (use rules slide) Go over the 5 Ups Rules.

Go over the *5 Ups Rules*: 1. Sit up straight. 2. Listen up. 3. Hush up. 4. Don't get up and run around or go to the bathroom. 5. Worship Up! (stand up and participate during praise and worship)

**Theme or Activity Songs:** Choose one or two fast-moving activity or theme songs that go with the curriculum.

**Game Time: Hopscotch Fear** (use game time slide)

*Supplies Needed:* rock, masking tape

*Preparation:* Use masking tape to make a hopscotch game on the floor. If you have too many students, make more than one game.

Have the students play traditional hopscotch, but call the rock the fear rock. To play hopscotch, have your students hop on one foot to each square and back. They must avoid the square with the fear rock on it.

*The easiest way to avoid fear in real life is to worship God.*

**Memory Verse Skit:** (use *Building a Fortress in God* Lesson 5, slide a and/or Kid James Skit #5 Video)

*Supplies needed:* Kid James Puppet (optional)

*Kid James:* Howdy, kids. I'm Kid James. I'm a Bible, but not just any Bible. I teach children the Word of God. Today's verse is about worship and how it helps us in times of trouble. Psalm 91:1-2 (NIV) says, *"Whoever dwells in the shelter of the Most High will rest in the shadow of the Almighty. I will say of the LORD, "He is my refuge and my fortress, my God, in whom I trust."*

God is bigger than any problem we face. When we worship Him, He fights our battles for us and we realize how great He is.

## Offering:

*Psalm 96:8 (NIV) says "Ascribe to the LORD the glory due his name; bring an offering and come into his courts." One way we worship God is by giving in the offering.*

## Skit: Sgt. Do Right Talks About Worship (optional - use Sgt. Do Right Skit #5 Video)

*Supplies Needed:* Army uniform (optional)

(Sgt. Do Right marches into the room and salutes.)

*Leader:* Hello, Sgt. Do Right.

*Sgt. Do Right:* Sgt. Do Right reporting as ordered, Sir (Ma'am). What spiritual weapon are we discussing today?

*Leader:* Today, we're talking about worship.

*Sgt. Do Right:* Worship? I don't understand. Last week, you taught that laughter fights spiritual battles, and now you're saying worship is a weapon?

*Leader:* That's right. Worship is one of the greatest spiritual weapons we have.

*Sgt. Do Right:* I agree that we should worship, and worship does make us feel good, but how is worship going to help us when we're going through a battle? What are we supposed to do, send the praise team into battle in front of the soldiers?

*Leader:* Absolutely. In fact, King Jehoshaphat did just that.

*Sgt. Do Right:* That poor deluded king. I imagine his army was slaughtered in a great defeat.

*Leader:* No, he won the battle, and not one of his soldiers was killed.

*Sgt. Do Right:* (shakes his head) How is that possible?

*Leader:* When we worship the Lord, first, we're acknowledging that God is bigger than our problems.

*Sgt. Do Right:* All right, Sir (Ma'am). It is true that God is bigger than any problem.

*Leader:* He's even bigger than any army.

*Sgt. Do Right:* I'll agree with that, Sir (Ma'am). But how can we fight with worship?

*Leader:* Because when we worship, God fights our battles for us. He will deliver us from any problems we have.

*Sgt. Do Right:* So ,what you're saying is, if we worship, we don't even have to stand against the enemy?

*Leader:* Oh, we still stand against the enemy, but we stand by worshipping.

*Sgt. Do Right:* You people fight battles using the weirdest weapons, Sir (Ma'am). I'm going to have to talk more about this with my captain.

(Salutes and exits)

**Verse of the Day: Psalm 91:1-2 (NIV)** *Whoever dwells in the shelter of the Most High will rest in the shadow of the Almighty. I will say of the LORD, "He is my refuge and my fortress, my God, in whom I trust."*

### Memory Verse Talk: (use *Building a Fortress in God* Lesson 5, slide a)

Have your students repeat the verse a couple of times.

*Have you ever heard the statement, "My praise is a weapon"? When we rest in the shadow of God by praising and worshipping Him, our praise does become a weapon because He is bigger than all our problems, and He will protect us and keep anything from harming us.*

### Memory Verse Activity: Memory Verse Bounce (use *Building a Fortress in God* Lesson 5, slide a)

Have your students stand in a circle facing each other. Have them repeat the verse several times. Then throw the ball to a student. Have him or her say the first word of the verse and throw the ball to another student who will say the next word. Repeat until the verse is recited several times. Make sure every student has at least one turn. If a student doesn't remember the next word of the verse, prompt him or her with the next word.

### Bible Story: Jehoshaphat and the Army of Worshippers

Supplies needed: crown (Burger King gives them away free), sign that says "Scared," sign that says "messenger," sign the says, "grrr," sign that says, "music," 2 hats or baseball caps, armor and swords (optional)

Choose a student to play Jehoshaphat. Have him or her wear a crown. Whenever you hold up the sign that says "scared" and point to the student, Jehoshaphat should act afraid and say, "Oh, no. We're doomed."

Choose a student to play Messenger. Have him or her wear the first hat. When you point to the messenger and hold up the "message" sign, the messenger pretends he or she is blowing a trumpet, says, "da, da, da da," and then says, "I have bad news."

Choose a student to play a priest named Jahaziel. Have him or her wear the second hat. When you point to Jahaziel and hold up the "message" sign, Jahaziel pretends he or she is blowing a trumpet, says, "do, do, da doo," and then says, "I have good news."

Depending on the size of your class, choose three to six students to play the bad guys for big, scary armies. Divide them up into three armies: the Moabites, the Ammonites, and the Meunites. If you have them available, give them armor and pretend swords. Whenever you hold up the "grrr" sign, have them growl.

Everyone else will play the people of Judah. When you hold up the "scared" sign, the students will say, "Oh, no. We're doomed." When you hold up the music sign, have your students sing the first line of the song, *My God is So Big*, or another song they know well.

Have each group practice their lines a couple of times. Encourage them to put feeling into their lines.

*Jehoshaphat was the king of Judah, and he loved God. He wanted everyone to love and follow God. One day, a messenger came.* Point to the messenger and hold up the "message" sign.

*The messenger told the king there were three armies that got together and were on their way to wipe out Judah.* Point to the armies and hold up the "grrr" sign.

Point to Jehoshaphat and hold up the "scared" sign. Point to the class and hold up the "scared" sign.

*Like I said before,* point the "grrr" sign at the armies, *the enemy was made up of three scary armies. They were the Moabites.* Point the "grrr" sign at Moabite actor. *The Ammonites.* Point "grrr" sign at Ammonites actor. *And the Meunites.* Point "grrr" sign at Meunite actor.

*As you can imagine, Jehoshaphat was freaking out.* Point "scared" sign at Jehoshaphat.

*Have you ever felt like that? Have you ever had a problem that seemed so much bigger than you? Like Jehoshaphat, maybe you were tempted to say...* Point "scared" sign at students.

*Jehoshaphat knew he was totally outnumbered. Judah didn't stand a chance. There was no way on earth he could beat this enemy. But Jehoshaphat knew God is bigger than any army, or even three armies! So he prayed.* Prompt Jehoshaphat to pretend to pray. *He also got the people of Judah to pray.* Have the students pretend to pray.

*Jehoshaphat prayed, "God, You're in charge of everything. You're bigger and more powerful than anyone. You defeated all our enemies in the past so please help us."*

*In 2 Chronicles 20:12 (NIV), he prayed, "For we have no power to face this vast army that is attacking us. We do not know what to do, but our eyes are on you." When Jehoshaphat was in trouble and scared,* hold up "scared" sign, *he decided to trust in God.*

*The people of Judah were scared too.* Point "scared" sign to students, *but they also trusted God.* Point music sign to students and Jehoshaphat and have them sing the praise chorus.

*After Jehoshaphat prayed, a priest named Jahaziel stood up and delivered a message from God.* Point "message" sign at Jahaziel. *In 2 Chronicles 20:15 (NIrV) Jahaziel said, "King, listen. The Lord says to you, 'Do not lose hope because of this vast army. The battle is not yours. It is God's.'" He told the king, "You're not going to have to fight. Just stand firm and watch what God can do."*

*The next day, Jehoshaphat trusted God so much that he put the worshippers at the head of the army. He knew when we worship, we are showing God we know He is bigger than all our fears.* Point music sign at students.

*At the very moment they begin to sing to God, God went after their enemies.*

*Now it was time for the big scary armies to be scared.* Point "scared" sign at armies. *It was time for them to say, "Oh, no. We're doomed."* Have the armies say that. Then have them act out the following scene.

*God confused the enemies. The Moabites and Ammonites began to fight the Meunites. After the Meunites were defeated, the Moabites and Ammonites turned and attacked each other. By the time Jehoshaphat's army arrived, those big, bad, terrifying armies were destroyed. God's people didn't have to fight at all.*

*When Jehoshaphat and his army saw what had happened, they praised God.* Point music sign at students, prompting them to sing praise chorus.

*When we worship God, we don't have to be afraid of any of the troubles that come against us. We are reminding ourselves that God is bigger than our problems, and He will fight our battle for us.*

**Praise and Worship**: Choose a couple of fast songs and a slow song to lead children into praise and worship. Include the praise chorus you sang during the Bible story. You can have a children's praise team, but until they understand leading praise and worship, have an adult leader or you be the worship leader.

## Object Lessons:

**1. Object Lesson: God is Bigger than My Problems** (Use *Building a Fortress in God* Lesson 5, slides b-g)

For each question, encourage your students to answer.

Show slide b. *Which is bigger, an elephant or a dog?*

Show slide c. *Which is bigger, an anthill or a house?*

Show slide d. *Which is bigger, a bear or a squirrel?*

Show slide e. *Which is bigger, a giraffe or a bumblebee?*

Show slide f. *Which is bigger, the universe or God?* If your students have trouble with this one, remind them that God made the universe.

Show slide g. *Which is bigger, your problems or God?*

*God made everything. He is bigger than any problem we could have. When we worship Him, He will fight our battles for us.*

**2. Object Lesson: Worship Gets Rid of Fear**

*Supplies needed:* dishwashing liquid, clear jar, clear pitcher of water, spoon, red food coloring, bowl or tray to catch water

Place a little water and a couple of tablespoons of dishwashing liquid in a jar and close the lid. Shake the jar as you are speaking until the jar fills with bubbles.

*There are a lot of things that can make us fearful. I'm afraid of...* (name a fear). *Everyone is afraid of something. What things are you afraid of?* Allow students to answer.

*Sometimes, people will try to tell you to just get over your fear. Does that help you stop being afraid? I sometimes try to tell myself that I shouldn't be afraid or there's nothing to be afraid of, but when I do, I get even more afraid. There is only one sure way to get rid of fear.*

Open the lid of the jar. Pour food coloring in the pitcher of water and stir it up. Then pour the colored water into the jar until all of the bubbles are gone and only the colored water remains. Do all of this while you are saying the following.

*When we are afraid, it can be a spiritual attack trying to convince us that the fear is bigger than God. It's hard to worship when we're afraid. But if we worship when we're afraid, we will begin to see that God is bigger than our fear and He will fight our battles for us. The more we worship, the more the worship will overcome our fear. Soon, there won't be any fear left.*

## Message: Earthquake Worship

*Supplies Needed:* earthquake sound effects (You can find this on music apps or on YouTube.)

*Paul and Silas were two disciples who were sharing the Gospel with others. As sometimes happens, people were angry with them because they were Christians and had them thrown in prison. The rulers had them beaten with whips before they threw them in a dark dungeon and placed chains on their wrists and ankles.*

*Have any of you ever had something really bad happen to you?* Allow students to answer. *What did you do when it happened? Sometimes people cry, or they get angry, or they hide, or they get really sad. All of those things are normal. It's all right to feel those emotions when something bad happens.*

*But that's not what Paul and Silas did. They sang worship songs to God. God must have been pleased with their worship because the next thing that happened was an earthquake.* Play earthquake music.

*Have you ever been in an earthquake?* Allow students to answer. *An earthquake can be a scary thing. It shakes everything up, even buildings.*

*This earthquake was so strong it opened all the prison doors, and the chains fell off all the prisoners, including Paul and Silas. The guard was afraid all the prisoners had escaped, but Paul and Silas told him not to worry. They were all there.*

*Then something really strange happened. The guard invited them to his house for dinner and asked them more about Jesus. He and his whole family were saved.*

*When something bad happens, there's nothing wrong with feeling scared, sad, or angry. But when we feel that way, we should also worship God. He is bigger than all our problems and will protect us and sometimes even send us an earthquake when we worship Him.*

For response time, encourage students to worship God.

## Small Group Activity: Extended Worship

*Supplies needed:* None

Encourage a time of extended worship. Ask students what their favorite worship songs in children's service are and play some of them during this time.

# Lesson 6 – Truth Matters (Belt of Truth)

**Focus Point:** God is always on the side of truth.

**Goal:** Students will learn that the truth matters because God is always on the side of truth. Lies and deception are against God.

**Verse of the Day: John 8:31b-32 (NIV)** *Jesus said, "If you hold to my teaching, you are really my disciples. Then you will know the truth, and the truth will set you free."*

**Supplies Needed:**

- *Building a Fortress in God* Downloadable Resources
- Kid James Puppet (optional)
- Army uniform costume for skit (optional)
- marker board
- marker
- sign with "lies" printed on it
- sign with "truth" printed on it
- regular man's belt
- decorative belt
- tool belt
- Roman soldier belt
- 2 brownies
- plant or flower
- Bible
- cards created from template in *Building a Fortress in God* Lesson 6 Truth Cards

**Opening:** *Building a Fortress in God Countdown* or *Building a Fortress in God* Slide (Available free with registration of this curriculum.)

**Welcome:** *Welcome to Building a Fortress in God. Today, we'll find out how truth matters to God. There are many deceptions and lies in this world. Some people will tell you there is no truth, or we can't know what's true. But God wants us to know what is true because truth matters to Him. That's why part of our spiritual armor is the belt of truth.*

**Prayer:** Ask a child to pray over the service. Encourage him or her to end the prayer with "In the Name of Jesus. Amen."

**Rules:** (use rules slide) Go over the 5 Ups Rules.

Go over the *5 Ups Rules*: 1. Sit up straight. 2. Listen up. 3. Hush up. 4. Don't get up and run around or go to the bathroom. 5. Worship Up! (stand up and participate during praise and worship)

**Theme or Activity Songs:** Choose one or two fast-moving activity or theme songs that go with the curriculum.

**Game Time: Numbers (**use game time slide)

*Supplies Needed:* None

Have students gather in a circle. Instruct them that when you call out a number, students should group in that number. For instance, if you call three, they should gather in groups of three. Students who fail to gather in the assigned number are out. Play until there are only a few students left. Then call a number that is one less than the number of students until there is only one or two students left and you have a winner.

*Some people say there is no truth or that truth doesn't matter. This game proves them wrong. When I called out a number, there was a right number that you had to gather into. That number was true. If you gathered in a different number, it was not the right number. It was false.*

**Memory Verse Skit:** (use *Building a Fortress in God* Lesson 6, slide a and/or Kid James Skit #5 Video)

*Supplies needed:* Kid James Puppet (optional)

*Kid James:* Howdy, kids. I'm Kid James. I'm a Bible, but not just any Bible. I teach children the Word of God. Today's verse is all about truth. If we follow Jesus Christ's teaching found in the Bible, we won't be confused by false teaching and the world's deceptions because we'll know the truth. John 31b-32 (NIV) says, "Jesus said, 'If you hold to my teaching, you are really my disciples. Then you will know the truth, and the truth will set you free.'" God's truth matters.

**Offering:**

*Do you know you can give an offering that God says is false. Mark 7:6-7 (NIV) says, "These people honor me with their lips, but their hearts are far from me. They worship me in vain; their teachings are merely human rules." In other words, if you do something to worship God, like give an offering, but you don't love God or want to honor Him, you just want to impress people, your offering is in vain. It's not a true offering which means it's false. It's good to give in the offering, but it's more important to give God our hearts.*

**Skit: Sgt. Do Right is Confused** (optional - use Sgt. Do Right Skit #6 Video)

*Supplies Needed:* Army uniform (optional)

(Sgt. Do Right marches into the room and salutes.)

*Leader:* Hello, Sgt. Do Right.

*Sgt. Do Right:* Hello, Sir (Ma'am). I was listening to what you were saying, and I'm a little confused.

*Leader:* Why are you confused, Sgt. Do Right?

*Sgt. Do Right:* Some of my fellow soldiers have been telling me some things about God that are completely different than what you're saying.

*Leader:* Like what?

*Sgt. Do Right:* One guy said there's no such thing as truth.

*Leader:* Is that true?

*Sgt. Do Right:* I don't know. That's what I'm asking you.

*Leader:* If there was no such thing as truth, then the statement that there is no such thing as truth wouldn't be true. Everyone, even those who don't follow God, know that some things are true and other things are not true.

*Sgt. Do Right:* (shakes his head) But another guy said God might be true for you, but my truth says there is no God.

*Leader:* Let me ask you something. What is two plus two?

*Sgt. Do Right:* Four.

*Leader:* What if I said that may be true for you, but my truth is it is five?

*Sgt. Do Right:* But that's not true. Two plus two is four for everybody.

*Leader:* That's right. There is no your truth or my truth. The truth is true for everybody. That means if God is real, which He is, He's real for everybody. And if Jesus died on the cross for our sins and rose again, that's true for everybody even if they choose not to believe it or accept God's forgiveness.

*Sgt. Do Right:* But some of the men asked how we know that God is real, and Jesus died on the cross and rose from the grave.

*Leader:* Some people would say you have to accept it by faith, and that is true. But there is a lot of scientific evidence that God created the universe. Even astronomers who don't believe in God admit the evidence points to a creator outside of the universe.

*Sgt. Do Right:* I didn't know that.

*Leader:* And did you know that there is more historical evidence that Jesus lived, died on the cross, and rose again than any other fact in history?

*Sgt. Do Right:* I didn't know that either. But does it really matter what we believe is the truth?

*Leader:* It matters very much. One of the most important pieces of our armor is the belt of truth. Only if we believe the truth can we have a relationship with God. Jesus said there is no other way to be saved except by Him. There is a lot of evidence that everything in the Bible is true, but I know God as my Lord and Savior, so I have faith in Him.

*Sgt. Do Right:* That's good to know. I guess I don't have enough faith to believe that God doesn't exist because God has shown Himself to me. I'm going to tell my fellow soldiers the truth. Bye.

(Salutes and exits)

## Verse of the Day: **John 8:31b-32 (NIV)** *Jesus said, "If you hold to my teaching, you are really my disciples. Then you will know the truth, and the truth will set you free."*

## Memory Verse Talk: (use *Building a Fortress in God* Lesson 6, slide a)

Have your students repeat the verse a couple of times.

*The truth is important, and the truth about God is the most important truth. That's why we need to believe every truth in the Bible. The truth will set us free from lies, the devil, and from sin. Truth matters.*

## Memory Verse Activity: Erase the Word

*Supplies needed:* Marker board, marker

*Preparation:* Write the verse on the marker board.

Have your students repeat the verse several times. Then erase a word and have them repeat the verse. Each time, erase another word and have the students say the verse until the board is empty.

## Bible Story: Adam and Eve Believe Lies and Jesus Defeats Lies

(Genesis 2-3; Matthew 4:1-11)

*Supplies needed:* sign with "lies" printed on it, sign with "truth" printed on it.

*Preparation:* Hang the "lies" sign on one side of the room and the "truth" sign on the other side of the room.

*Being able to distinguish lies from truth is an important tool in the Kingdom of God. That's why God gives His children the belt of truth. I'm going to tell two stories that are recorded in the Bible. Both of these stories are true, but in the stories, Satan, the father of lies, tries to trick the people involved. When I ask you to decide if something is true, run to the "truth" sign on the right or the "lies" sign on the left.*

*Let's try it out.* Say something that is obviously a lie like it is rainy when it is sunny or warm outside when it's cold. Encourage the students to pick a side. Praise them for choosing the correct side.

*The first story is about Adam and Eve. After God created them, He placed them in a garden called Eden to take care of the animals and crops. Is this true?* After the students choose sides, let them know it is indeed true. *In fact, our DNA proves we all descended from one man and one woman.* Have the students sit in the middle.

*That's when the serpent came in. At this point in the story, you might wonder how snakes can talk. Most snakes can't, but this was really Satan disguised as a snake.*

*The serpent was tricky. He asked Eve if God really said that if they ate from the fruit of the tree of the knowledge of good and evil, they would die. Eve said yes. She said God said they couldn't eat it or touch it. Is this true?* After the students choose sides, let them know it's only partly true. *God didn't say they couldn't touch it, only that they couldn't eat it. It was a trick question.* Both sides are partially right. Have the students sit.

*The serpent said, "You won't die. In fact, you'll become like God, knowing good and evil." Is this true?* After the students choose sides, let them know it's a lie. *Satan always lies. He tries to convince us that what God says is a lie, but he's the liar.* Have the students sit.

*At this point, Eve had a choice. She could believe the lies of the serpent, or she could believe what God says. Genesis 3:6 (NIV) says, "When the woman saw that the fruit of the tree was good for food and pleasing to the eye, and also desirable for gaining wisdom, she took some and ate it. She also gave some to her husband, who was with her, and he ate it."*

*When God came to the garden to walk with Adam and Eve, they hid because they were ashamed. Because of this lie, sin came into the world, and Adam and Eve eventually died. Is this true?* After the students choose sides, let them know it is true. Their sin caused separation from God. Have the students sit.

*When Jesus, the Son of God came into the world, He was fully God and fully man. Is this true?* After the students choose sides, let them know it is true.

*Jesus came to defeat sin, so He went in the desert to be tempted by Satan just as Adam and Eve were tempted. After Jesus fasted, went without food, for forty days, Satan showed up. The first thing Satan did was tempt Jesus to turn bread into stone. He knew Jesus had pledged to fast, so he tried to get Jesus to eat when He wasn't supposed to. Jesus, like Eve, went ahead and ate. Is this true?* After the students choose sides, let them know it is false. Have the students sit.

*Not only did Jesus refuse to eat, He used Scripture to declare truth to Satan. He said in Matthew 4:4 (NIV), "'Man shall not live by bread alone, but by every word that proceeds from the mouth of God.'" Basically, He said our relationship with God is more important than even what we eat.*

*Then Satan tried to tempt Jesus by daring Him to jump off a cliff. Satan told Him it would be all right since He was God, and angels would protect Him. In this case, Satan was telling the truth but for a false reason. He wanted Jesus to accept his dare and be guilty of pride. Jesus knew better and declared Scripture again. In Matthew 4:7 NIV, Jesus said, "You shall not tempt the Lord your God." Kids sometimes will dare you to do foolish things. When they do that, remember that Satan tried the same thing with Jesus. Don't give in to it.*

*The third way Satan tempted Jesus was to promise Him all the treasure the world had to offer. All Jesus had to do was bow down and worship Satan. Do you think Satan was telling the truth?* After the students choose sides, let them know Satan was telling a partial truth. *He is called the god of this world, and he did have access to treasures, but Jesus is God. He owns everything. He came to Earth as a man so He could face Satan's lies and declare the truth. Once He did that, He could redeem all of us on the cross and rise again, defeating death. Jesus knew this and declared the truth of Scripture again. In Matthew 4:10 NIV, he said, "Away with you, Satan! For it is written, 'You shall worship the Lord your God, and Him only you shall serve.'"*

*Because of Jesus, our relationship with God can be restored when we give our lives to Him. We can defeat Satan's lies by declaring the truth. We can find the truth in God's Word.*

**Praise and Worship**: Choose a couple of fast songs and a slow song to lead children into praise and worship. You can have a children's praise team, but until they understand leading praise and worship, have an adult leader or you be the worship leader.

## Object Lessons:

**1. Object Lesson: Special Belts** (Use *Building a Fortress in God* Video Lesson 6, *Batman's Utility Belt*)

Supplies Needed: regular man's belt, decorative belt, tool belt, Roman soldier belt

(optional) Use *Building a Fortress in God* Lesson 6 slides b-e as an option instead of the various belts in the supplies needed list.

*Today, we're talking about a belt, specifically the Belt of Truth, so I thought I'd show you these belts and discuss what they're used for.* Show man's belt or slide b. *What do you think this belt is used for?* Allow students to answer. *That's right. This is a belt to hold up a man's pants. Sometimes, if a man doesn't wear a belt, his pants might fall down and everyone will see what kind of underwear he has on. He'll be showing something he shouldn't. The belt of truth also holds up what is true and right. Without it, nobody would know if something is right or wrong, and everybody would be doing things they shouldn't.*

Show decorative belt or slide c. *This is a decorative belt that women sometimes wear. Do you think this belt is going to hold up anyone's pants?* Allow students to answer. *Of course not. It's used for decoration. Another word for that is adornment. In Titus 2:9 (NKJV), it says, "that they may adorn the doctrine of God our Savior in all things." The doctrine of God is the truth. The belt of truth adorns us with the truth of God.*

Show tool belt or slide d. *This is a tool belt. What is it used for?* Allow students to answer. *That's right. People use it to hold their tools while they're working so they don't have to constantly go get the tools they need. The belt of truth holds the knowledge of God. It has the tools you need to help you know if something is true or false. The main tools in the belt of truth are the Bible, prayer, and the Holy Spirit on the inside of you. Sometimes, lies try to fool you by adding part of the truth to them. When something is part true and part false, it is still a lie. By using the tools in the belt of truth, you'll be able to discern what is true, what is partly true, and what is a lie.*

Show *Building a Fortress in God* Lesson 6, *Batman's Utility Belt* video.

*Batman's utility belt is amazing. It's not only a tool belt, but it holds everything you can imagine to get Batman out of any trouble the bad guys get him into. The belt of truth will also protect you in times of danger by helping you know what the right thing to do is.*

Show Roman soldier's belt or side e. *This belt is part of the armor of a Roman soldier. Its main purpose was to hold the sword and dagger. All the other pieces of armor attached to the belt so they would stay in place. It would be made of brass and would cover the lower body to protect it. It was very important for a soldier to have his belt. The belt of truth is the first piece of armor in the armor of God. The truth holds everything in place. It keeps us from shifting from truth into deception just as the Roman belt keeps the pieces of armor from shifting. The truth protects us from all the lies that would try to convince us not to believe God and His Word. It also holds the Sword of the Spirit which is the Word of God and shows us the Bible is always true.*

## 2. Object Lesson: A Little Lie Spoils the Truth

*Supplies needed:* 2 brownies

Choose a student. If you like, ask questions about the lesson so far to choose which student.

*I made these brownies myself. This brownie,* point to the brownie on the right, *has all the important ingredients to make a good brownie. It has flour, sugar, chocolate chips, milk, butter, and some other wholesome ingredients. But I wanted to do something different with this brownie,* point to the brownie on the left. *I added just a little bit of dog poop for flavoring.*

*So which brownie do you want?* Allow the student to choose. Occasionally, the child will choose the brownie on the left as a joke. Encourage the student to choose the brownie on the right or choose another student to make the choice. *Are you sure you want that brownie? There's only a little dog poop in this other brownie.* Allow the student to eat the brownie. Then eat the other brownie. The students will probably make a commotion about this.

*I was lying when I said there was dog poop in the brownie I ate. I'm sorry I lied to you. I was making a point that even a little dog poop would ruin the brownie. If someone tells part of the truth but adds a little bit that isn't the truth, it ruins everything they said. If there's even a little bit of lie, like when I said there was dog poop in the brownie, it is a lie.*

### Message: What is Truth (Use *Building a Fortress in God* Lesson 6, slides f - i)

Supplies needed: plant or flower, Bible

Show slide f. *In John 18:38 (NIV) a Roman governor named Pilate asked Jesus, "What is truth?" Today, people are still asking that question. Truth is something that is real or fact. It's also something that is consistent with God. God is truth.*

Show a plant or flower. *The truth of God is revealed in nature. All you have to do is look at a sunrise or a sunset to know there is a Creator who created everything. Do you know even astronomers admit that something outside the universe created the universe? That Creator is God.*

Show slide g. *Jesus is truth and the only way to God. In John 14:6 (NIV), Jesus said, "I am the way, the truth, and the life. No one can come to the Father except through me." If anyone tells you it doesn't matter what you believe, that's not true.*

Show slide h and Bible. *God's word is Truth. Historical evidence and archeological digs prove Scripture. There has never been an archeological dig that has disproven something in the Bible.*

*The Holy Spirit leads us to truth.*

Show slide i. *John 16:13 (NIV) says, "When the Spirit of truth comes, he will guide you into all truth."*

*God wants you to speak the truth and to know the truth. That's why He gives those who follow Him the Belt of Truth. The truth matters to God, so it should matter to us.*

During response time, pray and anoint each student. Pray for them to be protected from the lies of the enemy.

### Small Group Activity: Truth Cards

*Supplies needed:* Cards created from template in *Building a Fortress in God* Lesson 6 Truth Cards

Read the front of each card. Allow your students to determine if the card is true or false. Then read the verse on the back of the card.

# Lesson 7 – I Can Pray When I'm In Trouble (Breastplate of Righteousness)

**Focus Point:** I can pray when I'm in trouble because I'm right with God.

**Goal:** Students will learn that whatever problems they are having, even if it's their fault, they can pray and ask God to deliver them because He is their righteousness.

**Verse of the Day: Psalm 91:15 (NIV)** *He will call on me, and I will answer him; I will be with him in trouble, I will deliver him and honor him.*

**Supplies Needed:**

- *Building a Fortress in God* Downloadable Resources
- Kid James Puppet (optional)
- Army uniform costume for skit (optional)
- picture of a hen and her chicks (optional – a real baby chick)
- umbrella
- colorful cardstock (1 for each student)
- glue
- feathers
- stickers
- crayons
- glitter

**Opening:** *Building a Fortress in God Countdown* or *Building a Fortress in God* Slide (Available free with registration of this curriculum.)

**Welcome:** *Welcome to Building a Fortress in God. Today, we're going to talk about a piece of armor every Christian wears. It's the breastplate of righteousness. When you ask Jesus into your heart, He gives you His righteousness. That means you are always right with God. Because you are right with God, you can pray to Him whenever you're in trouble, and He will deliver you.*

**Prayer:** Ask a child to pray over the service. Encourage him or her to end the prayer with "In the Name of Jesus. Amen."

**Rules:** (use rules slide) Go over the 5 Ups Rules.

Go over the *5 Ups Rules*: 1. Sit up straight. 2. Listen up. 3. Hush up. 4. Don't get up and run around or go to the bathroom. 5. Worship Up! (stand up and participate during praise and worship)

**Theme or Activity Songs:** Choose one or two fast-moving activity or theme songs that go with the curriculum.

### Game Time: Surrounded by Righteousness (use game time slide)

*Supplies Needed:* None

Choose one student to be it and another student to be protected. The protected student stands in the center. The it student stands outside the circle. The rest of the students stand in a tight circle, locking arms, to protect the student. The student who is it tries to touch the protected student. The students in the circle can avoid the it student by moving and maneuvering but can't unlock their arms. If the it student touches the protected student, that student gets to be the protected student, and another student is it. If you have a lot of students, you may want to divide them into multiple circles to keep the circles smaller.

*As difficult as it was for the student who was it to get to the protected student, it's even harder for trouble to destroy a child of God protected by God's righteousness.*

### Memory Verse Skit: (use *Building a Fortress in God* Lesson 7, slide a and/or Kid James Skit #7 Video)

*Supplies needed:* Kid James Puppet (optional)

*Kid James:* Howdy, kids. I'm Kid James. I'm a Bible, but not just any Bible. I teach children the Word of God. Today's verse is about calling out to God in times of trouble. Psalm 91:15 (NIV) says, *"He will call on me, and I will answer him; I will be with him in trouble, I will deliver him and honor him."*

Because God protects our hearts with the breastplate of His righteousness, we can call on Him in times of trouble, and He will deliver us.

### Offering:

*Proverbs 11:25 (ICB) says "A person who gives to others will get richer. Whoever helps others will himself be helped." Have any of you ever known a stingy person? Stingy people don't help others, and when offering time comes, they don't want to give even though they know this offering goes to help* (Name what the offering goes toward.) *This verse talks about generous people who give to others. I know most of you are very generous and like to help others.* If you have an example of your students being generous or helping others, commend them for it. *This verse says when you give generously, you will get more to give. If you help others, people will help you when you need help.*

### Skit: Sgt. Do Right Talks About His Troubles (optional - use Sgt. Do Right Skit #7 Video)

*Supplies Needed:* Army uniform (optional)

(Sgt. Do Right marches into the room and salutes.)

*Leader:* Hello, Sgt. Do Right.

*Sgt. Do Right:* Sgt. Do Right reporting as ordered, Sir (Ma'am). I can't stay long today.

*Leader:* What's the matter, Sgt. Do Right? You look like you're in trouble.

*Sgt. Do Right:* I am, Sir (Ma'am). I'm in big trouble. The captain ordered me to make sure the Jeeps are in working order. I had twenty Jeeps to service, and I've finished nineteen. But the last Jeep won't start no matter how hard I try. I tried changing the battery and the starter, but it seems no matter what I do, I can't get it working. I'm supposed to be done by tomorrow, and the captain's going to be plenty mad at me. He might make me do one hundred push-ups, or worse.

*Leader:* I'm sorry to hear that. Today, we're talking about a piece of God's armor that can protect us when we're in trouble.

*Sgt. Do Right:* Armor might help in battle, but I doubt you have a piece of armor that will protect me from the captain when he gets angry.

*Leader:* Are you a child of God?

*Sgt. Do Right:* Yes, I am. I've asked Jesus into my heart as my Savior.

*Leader:* Then you're already protected by the breastplate of righteousness. You can call on God when you're in trouble.

*Sgt. Do Right:* I'm all for prayer, but I don't see how that will help.

*Leader:* When you become a Christian, you receive the breastplate of righteousness. That means you're right with God. When you call upon Him in times of trouble, He protects you just as the breastplate in armor protects a soldier from injury to his heart.

*Sgt. Do Right:* (shakes his head) I don't see how God could protect me this time. How would God help me fix a Jeep? I mean, He isn't going to come down here and point to the part that's broken.

*Leader:* God could do that, but He's more likely to guide you to the problem with the Jeep.

*Sgt. Do Right:* Do you think God would do that?

*Leader:* He might. Or He might just make the Jeep start on its own.

*Sgt. Do Right:* That would be awesome. I'm going to pray for Him to do that right now.

*Leader:* Just a sec. I said He could do that, but you have to let God decide how He wants to help you. He might decide to help you tell the captain the truth, and the captain might understand.

*Sgt. Do Right:* You don't know my captain.

*Leader:* Your captain's no match for my God. But there are many other ways He could help you get out of this trouble, or He might even give you peace and joy while you're doing those push-ups. God might even want you to do push-ups to make you stronger.

*Sgt. Do Right:* I'll call on the Lord and let Him decide how to help me. I have to go work on the Jeep some more. Bye.

(Salutes and exits)

### Verse of the Day: **Psalm 91:15 (NIV)** *He will call on me, and I will answer him; I will be with him in trouble, I will deliver him and honor him.*

### Memory Verse Talk: (use *Building a Fortress in God* Lesson 7, slide a)

Have your students repeat the verse a couple of times.

*When something bad happens, what should you do?* Allow students to answer. Acknowledge their answers. If nobody says it, add "call out to God in prayer." *God is our breastplate of righteousness. When we become Christians, we are right with God. That means whatever trouble we face, we can call out to God, and He will protect us. So, when you're in trouble, what should you do?* Allow students to answer "call out to God."

### Memory Verse Activity: Clap a Word (use *Building a Fortress in God* Lesson 7, slide a)

Choose one student to be it. That student must leave the room with a volunteer. Have the students rehearse the verse but clap instead of saying the word "shelter." When the student comes back, the other students say the verse, and the student who is it must say which word was clapped.

If you have time, you can repeat this activity by choosing another student to be it and another word to be clapped.

### Bible Story: King Saul Hunts David (use *Building a Fortress in God* Lesson 7, slides b-f)

(1 Samuel 23)

Show slide b. *Back in Bible days, Israel had a wicked king named Saul. God rejected Saul as king and had a prophet named Samuel anoint the next king, David. You may remember David as the shepherd boy who fought the giant, Goliath, and won. David knew he was the next king, but he wasn't king yet. He would wait for God to remove Saul before he became king.*

*David did everything to serve King Saul, but the king was jealous. He wanted his son to be the next king, not David. He planned to kill David, so David ran. David was in a lot of trouble, but he knew what to do.*

Show slide c. *Once, David and his men were in a fortified city, and he heard Saul was plotting to get him. He went to a priest named Abithar and asked for the ephod. An ephod is a square piece of material with twelve gems on it to represent the twelve tribes of Israel. The priest would wear it over his chest just as we wear the breastplate of righteousness over our chests to protect our hearts. In those days, Israelites would wear it when they were calling out to God. That's what David did. God warned David that the men of the city would turn him over to Saul, so he and his men escaped.*

Show slide d. *David kept running from place to place to avoid Saul, but he kept calling on God to help him. Once, when he was in Horesh, Saul's son Jonathan warned him Saul was coming and encouraged him. Even though Jonathan was Saul's son, he was a good friend to David.*

Show slide e. *Another time, David was hiding in the desert mountains. Saul was going along one side of the mountain, and David was going up the other side. Saul and his men were about to capture David. David must have been really scared.*

Show slide f. *In Psalm 59:1 (NIV), he prayed, "Deliver me from my enemies, O God; be my fortress against those who are attacking me." God came to the rescue. A messenger came to Saul and told him the Philistines were invading Israel. Saul broke off the search for David right before he would have caught him and went to battle with the Philistines.*

*Even though Saul kept chasing David, because David trusted in the Lord and called out to him, God protected him. A few years later, Saul died in battle and David became king.*

*David knew he could call on God in times of trouble when he was in danger. He continued to trust God and call on Him whenever he or the people of Israel were in trouble. Because of this, God called him a man after His own heart. We can also call out to God in prayer when we're in trouble because we are right with God.*

**Praise and Worship:** Choose a couple of fast songs and a slow song to lead children into praise and worship. You can have a children's praise team, but until they understand leading praise and worship, have an adult leader or you be the worship leader.

## Object Lessons:

**1. Object Lesson: The Breastplate of Righteousness** (Use *Building a Fortress in God* Lesson 7 slide g

*How many of you have ever heard of a bulletproof vest?* Allow students to answer.

Show slide g. *A bulletproof vest is a modern-day breastplate. In Bible days, soldier wore heavy metal breastplates to protect their hearts, lungs, and other vital organs from attacks from swords, arrows, and other weapons. If a bad guy stabbed a soldier in the heart and he didn't have a breastplate on, what would happen?* Allow students to answer that the soldier would probably die.

*Today, soldiers don't use swords or arrows to fight battles, and police usually aren't attacked by bad guys using swords. What is the weapon most bad guys use today?* Allow students to answer. If nobody mentions it, suggest guns or knives. *Bad guys use guns or knives today.*

*A bulletproof vest is worn by soldiers and police to protect their hearts, lungs, and vital organs. If a bad guy shoots a police officer or a soldier, a bulletproof vest can save their lives.*

*When we accept Jesus as our Savior, we are given a spiritual bulletproof vest called the breastplate of righteousness. This means our hearts are protected because we are right with God. Even though we have done wrong things in our lives, we are right with God because Jesus, who has never sinned or done anything wrong, becomes our righteousness. He protects us from the results of sin.*

*Because of this, we can call on the Lord whenever we're in trouble, and He will protect us. People who aren't Christian can't do that, because they aren't right with God.*

*But what happens when we sin? What if we are in trouble because we've done wrong? Do we still have on the breastplate of righteousness? David faced a problem like this. He romanced a woman who was someone else's wife. When he did this, he sinned against God. He was in a lot of trouble because of it. But David still called out to God. He asked God to forgive him and take away his sin. He deserved death for what he did, but he still had on the breastplate of righteousness because he still trusted God to save him from his sin. God protected him and saved him from the death sentence. He still had consequences for his sin, but he was right with God.*

*When we are in the wrong and have sinned against God, we still have Jesus' righteousness protecting us. We need to ask God's forgiveness, and He will forgive us. We won't ever lose our breastplate of righteousness as long as we continue to call out to God. He will still deliver us in times of trouble.*

## 2. Object Lesson: A Mother Hen

*Supplies needed:* picture of a hen and her chicks (optional – a real baby chick)

Nobody's sure where this story originated. It might be true, but there have been many versions told, so it's hard to know.

*A long time ago, on a farm far from here, there was a mother hen with a number of baby chicks. She took good care of them. She fed them and cleaned their feathers. At night, she would hide them under her wings to protect them from the cold night air. One night, there was a fire on the farm. The mother hen knew she could get away from the fire in time, but her chicks were little and moved too slowly. The fire got closer and closer to the hen house. The mother hen decided what she needed to do. She hid all of the chicks under her wings to protect them from the fire. As the fire got closer, it became hotter and hotter for the mother hen, but she didn't move. The fire killed the hen that night, but the farmer found the chicks under their mother's wings. They were alive and well.*

*The Bible describes God's protection in Psalm 91:4 (NIV). He will cover you with his feathers, and under his wings you will find refuge; his faithfulness will be your shield and rampart.*

## Message: God Protects Me when I call to Him

*Supplies Needed:* umbrella

Show closed umbrella. *What am I holding?* Allow students to answer.

*What is this umbrella used for?* Allow students to answer. Some answers might be protection from rain or shade from the hot sun.

*If I never open the umbrella, will it protect me from rain or sun?* Allow students to answer.

*In order to use this umbrella, I need to open it.* Open the umbrella.

*God is like an umbrella protecting us from danger and trouble if we are His children, but we have an obligation to call to Him in prayer when that happens. Praying to God for help is like opening an umbrella.*

*In Psalm 91, it lists some of the things God protects us from.*

*In verse 3, He'll protect us from hidden dangers and traps we don't even know about. Sometimes, He might put something in our paths to keep us from doing something we want to do because there is a danger there we don't know about.*

*In verses six through eight, He also protects us from dangers we do know about and gives us peace. Some of the dangers it mentions are war or diseases like Covid or other viruses.*

*In verses 9 through 13, God protects our families and us against any harm that comes our way. He will even send His angels to guard us and our homes.*

*In verse fourteen, He promises to rescue us because He loves us, but in verse fifteen, He tells us what He wants us to do when we're in trouble.*

*Psalm 91:15 (NIV) says, "He will call on me, and I will answer him; I will be with him in trouble, I will deliver him and honor him."*

For response time, ask if any students need prayer for troubles in their lives. Anoint and pray for them. During worship time, anoint and pray for the protection of every student.

## Small Group Craft: Psalm 91:15 Verse

*Supplies needed:* Colorful cardstock (1 for each student), glue, feathers, stickers, crayons, glitter

*Preparation:* Print the Bible verse on each sheet of cardstock. If using a printer, you can find a copy of it in *Building a Fortress in God* Lesson 6, picture 1. Lay out feathers and other decorations for student to decorate their cardstock verses. Remind them that the feathers are to remind them that God will cover them with His feathers to protect them.

# Lesson 8 – God Gives Me the Words to Say (Shoes of the Gospel of Peace)

**Focus Point:** When you're sharing with others about God, He will give you the words to say.

**Goal:** Students will learn that God helps them say the right thing when they share about God with others.

**Verse of the Day: Luke 12:12 (NIV)** *For the Holy Spirit will teach you at that time what you should say.*

**Supplies Needed:**

- *Building a Fortress in God* Downloadable Resources
- Kid James Puppet (Optional)
- Army uniform costume for skit (optional)
- strips of paper
- scissors
- tape
- chairs
- Legos
- rainboots
- snow boots
- tennis shoes
- sandals
- clear bowl
- whole milk
- food coloring
- dishwashing liquid
- 2 cotton swabs
- colorful cardstock (1 for each student)
- marker
- scissors
- crayons
- stickers
- hole punch
- ribbons

**Opening:** *Building a Fortress in God Countdown* or *Building a Fortress in God* Slide (Available free with registration of this curriculum.)

**Welcome:** *Welcome to Building a Fortress in God. Not only does God help us in times of trouble, but He also teaches us what to say when we share the Good News of Jesus Christ.*

**Prayer:** Ask a child to pray over the service. Encourage him or her to end the prayer with "In the Name of Jesus. Amen."

**Rules:** (use rules slide) Go over the 5 Ups Rules.

Go over the *5 Ups Rules*: 1. Sit up straight. 2. Listen up. 3. Hush up. 4. Don't get up and run around or go to the bathroom. 5. Worship Up! (stand up and participate during praise and worship)

**Theme or Activity Songs:** Choose one or two fast-moving activity or theme songs that go with the curriculum.

**Game Time: Charades** (use game time slide)

*Supplies Needed:* none

Have your students group into teams of four to six students. The team that goes first gets to choose one team member to go first. That team member will decide the word or phrase. The team member will act out the word or phrase without using words. The first team has one minute to guess the phrase. Then each team has a turn to do the same thing.

**Memory Verse Skit:** (use *Building a Fortress in God* Lesson 8, slide a and/or Kid James Skit #8 Video)

*Supplies needed:* Kid James Puppet (optional)

*Kid James:* Howdy, kids. I'm Kid James. I'm a Bible, but not just any Bible. I teach children the Word of God. God wants everyone to hear the Good News about how Jesus died on the cross and rose again so they can be saved. The way He does that is by having His children share the good news. Sometimes, it's hard to know what to say when you share about Jesus to your friends and family. That's what today's memory verse is all about. Luke 12:12 (NIV) says, "For the Holy Spirit will teach you at that time what you should say." Don't worry about what to say when you talk to people about God. The Holy Spirit will help you.

## Offering:

*Romans 10:14-15 (NIV) says, "How, then, can they call on the one they have not believed in? And how can they believe in the one of whom they have not heard? And how can they hear without someone preaching to them? And how can anyone preach unless they are sent? As it is written: 'How beautiful are the feet of those who bring good news!'" One way we share the Good News of Jesus Christ is to give an offering to support missionaries who go to places around the world to share the Gospel with other nations and peoples.*

This would be a good time to talk about a missionary your church supports.

**Skit: Sgt. Do Right's Shoes** (optional - use Sgt. Do Right Skit #8 Video)

*Supplies Needed:* Army uniform (optional)

(Sgt. Do Right marches into the room and salutes.)

*Leader:* Hello, Sgt. Do Right.

*Sgt. Do Right:* Sgt. Do Right reporting as ordered, Sir (Ma'am). I'm having a hard time figuring out today's armor.

*Leader:* What do you mean?

*Sgt. Do Right:* Well, Sir (Ma'am). We're supposed to have our shoes fitted with the readiness of the Gospel of Peace. I understand the shoes part. Army boots are very important to a soldier. They have to be comfortable so the soldier can march for a long time, and they have to be waterproof so the soldier's feet don't get wet and strong so they don't wear out easily.

*Leader:* That's all true. If you understand that, what part are you having trouble with.

*Sgt. Do Right:* A few things, Sir (Ma'am). First of all, what does the readiness mean?

*Leader:* That part is easy. A soldier has to be ready at all times.

*Sgt. Do Right:* That's true. I guess I get your meaning about that, but what does the Gospel of Peace mean?

*Leader:* Gospel means the good news that Jesus Christ died on the cross for our sins so we can be right with God. When we're right with God, we have peace.

*Sgt. Do Right:* (shakes his head) But how can we be ready with the Gospel of Peace? Don't we already have that good news when we're saved?

*Leader:* Yes, we do. But others around us need to know the Good News about Jesus. How can they know about the Gospel of Peace unless we go and tell them?

*Sgt. Do Right:* That's a good point. I guess they're called shoes because we're supposed to go and tell people about the Good News of Jesus Christ.

*Leader:* Now you understand.

*Sgt. Do Right:* That creates a bit of a problem. When I'm nervous, I sometimes get tongue-tied and don't know what to say. How will I tell people about Jesus then?

*Leader:* The Bible gives us more good news about that. When we tell others about Jesus, the Holy Spirit will teach us what to say and when to say it.

*Sgt. Do Right:* Wow, that is good news. I'm going to tell all the men in my platoon about Jesus. I have to run now. I'm going to go and tell the Good News. Bye.

(Salutes and exits)

**Verse of the Day: Luke 12:12 (NIV)** *For the Holy Spirit will teach you at that time what you should say.*

**Memory Verse Talk:** (use *Building a Fortress in God* Lesson 8, slide a)

Have your students repeat the verse a couple of times.

*Sometimes, it's hard to share Jesus with your friends because you don't know what to say or how they'll react. That's why today's memory verse is so important. When you are ready to share with your friends, ask God what to say. The Holy Spirit will give you the words. The more you rely on the Holy Spirit to do this, the easier it will become.*

**Memory Verse Activity: Random Chairs Verse**

*Supplies needed:* strips of paper, scissors, tape, chairs

*Preparation:* Print the verse on paper. Cut the paper into strips so there will be one word or phrase on each strip. Tape the strips to the bottom of random chairs the students will sit on.

Have your students repeat the verse a couple of times.

Tell your students that some of the chairs have pieces of paper taped to them. Tell them to look under their chairs. The students with pieces of paper will come to the front. Have them arrange the strips of paper to reveal the verse.

**Video: Armor of God** (Use *Building a Fortress in God* Video Lesson 8 *Armor of God*)

**Bible Story: Peter and John Talk to Religious Leaders**

(Acts 4:1-22)

*A few weeks ago, we learned about the lame man who was healed when Peter and John prayed for him. He was so excited. He went walking, and leaping, and praising God. Today, we're going to learn the rest of the story.*

*The people were astonished about this man being healed, so Peter and John told them the Good News about Jesus Christ. God gave them the words to say so the crowd would listen.*

*When the religious leaders heard what Peter and John said, they were angry. They didn't believe Jesus was God, and they wanted to stop what Peter and John were preaching. They had the two disciples arrested and brought before them.*

*The High Priest questioned them and said, "By what power and name do you heal people?"*

*The Holy Spirit didn't only give Peter and John the words when they were sharing the Gospel,*

He also gave them the right words when they were in danger. *Acts 4 says Peter was filled with the Holy Spirit and told the leaders they healed by the name of Jesus Christ whom the religious leaders had killed, and that Jesus rose from the dead.*

*In Acts 4:12 (NIV), Peter said, "Salvation is found in no one else, for there is no other name under heaven given to mankind by which we must be saved."*

*The religious leaders were surprised that these men with no education could speak so boldly. They realized that these men had been with Jesus. But they hated Jesus and ordered the men to stop preaching and healing in His name.*

*Sometimes when you share the Gospel of Jesus Christ, some people won't like it. That's okay. Scripture tells us not everyone wants to be saved, but you still should be ready to tell them about Jesus.*

*Peter and John said they would continue to preach in Jesus' name because they would obey God rather than man. Even though the religious leaders were angry, they released Peter and John. The disciples continued to tell everyone about Jesus, and the Holy Spirit gave them the words to say.*

**Praise and Worship**: Choose a couple of fast songs and a slow song to lead children into praise and worship. You can have a children's praise team, but until they understand leading praise and worship, have an adult leader or you be the worship leader.

## Object Lessons:

**1. Object Lesson: Shoes are Important** (Use *Building a Fortress in God* Lesson 8, slide b)

*Supplies Needed:* Legos, rainboots, snow boots, tennis shoes, sandals

*Shoes are important.* Show Legos. *If you don't believe me, try stepping on one of these in your bare feet. Before we talk about shoes that are part of the armor of God, let me show you a few other pairs of shoes.*

Show rainboots. *What are these?* Allow students to answer. *Rainboots are important to wear if you're outside and it is raining. There are a lot of muddy puddles you might step in, and your shoes would get all muddy and wet. They are also important to wear if you want to jump in muddy puddles. As Peppa Pig always says, "If you want to jump in muddy puddles, you must wear your boots."*

Show snow boots. *These are another pair of boots. When do you wear these?* Allow students to answer. *You wear snow boots when it is very cold and snowy outside. The warm lining,* show lining, *keeps your feet warm and dry, and the boots are high enough to keep any snow from getting in your boots and making your feet cold and wet.*

Show tennis shoes. *I'm sure most of you have a pair of tennis shoes. Some of you are even wearing them today. Why would we wear tennis shoes?* Allow students to answer. Suggest the following answers if nobody has said them: comfortable, easy to walk or run in, can wear on gym floors, protect feet if you step on something like a Lego.

Show sandals. *Why would you wear a pair of sandals?* Allow students to answer. Suggest the following answers if nobody has said them: comfortable, keeps feet cool on hot days, airy, protects feet if you step on hot cement, bugs, bees, or Legos.

Show slide b. *This is a pair of Roman solider shoes. These are Roman military boots/sandals from Bible times. They were called caligae. The sole had hobnails on the bottom to have better traction in the desert sands. They had straps to make them sandals because it would get hot, and also so they could adjust the straps to fit each foot, making them more comfortable to wear. Comfort was important because these soldiers had to walk miles with no rest. These were the shoes Paul would have thought of when he told Christians in Ephesians 6:15 (NIV) to have "our feet fitted with the readiness that comes from the gospel of peace."*

*The idea is we are always ready to share the Gospel. We may have to travel to share with people or we might just have to stand still. The hobnails on the bottom help us stand firm while sharing about Jesus to others. The airy straps that make the shoes comfortable remind us that the Holy Spirit will give us the right words to say and keep us in peace with God.*

## 2. Object Lesson: Milking the Gospel

*Supplies needed:* clear bowl, whole milk, food coloring, dishwashing liquid, 2 cotton swabs

*Preparation:* Do this experiment at home first to determine how it works. Use whole milk because the fat in the milk makes the experiment work.

*It is difficult to share the Gospel of Jesus Christ on our own.* Pour enough milk into the bowl to cover it around a ½ inch deep. *The milk represents the world.* Add 4 drops of food coloring. *The food coloring represents the Gospel. I might try to share the Gospel alone with the world.* Swirl the food coloring around with a cotton swab. *No matter how hard I try, it doesn't work.*

*But Jesus promised the Holy Spirit would help me by giving me the right words to say and helping me know when to say them. That's why I wear the shoes of the readiness of the Gospel of Peace.* Dip the second cotton swab in dishwashing liquid. *The dishwashing liquid represents the power of the Holy Spirit within me. Watch what happens.* Swirl the cotton swab around in the food coloring. The coloring should mix with the milk this time.

*When we ask the Holy Spirit to help us to share the Gospel, we are putting on the shoes of the readiness of the Gospel of Peace. He will teach us what to say and when to say it.*

## Message: God Gives Me the Words When I'm sharing the Gospel:

*Have you ever tried to tell people about Jesus, but you got nervous and tongue-tied? It's difficult*

*to share the Gospel without the power of the Holy Spirit. When we receive the baptism of the Holy Spirit, He teaches our tongue to speak in a heavenly language, but He also teaches us what to say and when to say it. He is our shoes of the Gospel of Peace.*

*In Acts 1:8 (NIrV), Jesus said, "But you will receive power when the Holy Spirit comes on you. Then you will tell people about me in Jerusalem, and in all Judea and Samaria. And you will even tell other people about me from one end of the earth to the other."*

*The power of the Holy Spirit will help you know what to say and when to say it when you tell others about Jesus.*

*When I'm in Danger: In Luke 12:11-12 (NIV), Jesus said, "When you are brought before synagogues, rulers and authorities, do not worry about how you will defend yourselves or what you will say, for the Holy Spirit will teach you at that time what you should say."*

*The Holy Spirit doesn't only teach us what to say when we share the Gospel, He will tell us what to say when we're in danger. Just as Peter and John knew what to say when they came before the rulers, the Holy Spirit will teach you what to say in dangerous situations. He'll show you what to say when a bully picks on you. He'll show you what to say when a teacher tells you you're not allowed to pray at school or believe what the Bible says. He'll even show you what to say when students or family come against you because you've made a stand for Jesus Christ. You can always trust the Holy Spirit to give you the right words to say.*

*He gives me peace. The Holy Spirit doesn't only give us the words to say, He keeps us in peace in difficult times. John 14:26-27 (NIV) says, "But the Advocate, the Holy Spirit, whom the Father will send in my name, will teach you all things and will remind you of everything I have said to you. Peace I leave with you; my peace I give you. I do not give to you as the world gives. Do not let your hearts be troubled and do not be afraid."*

*We can trust the Holy Spirit to give us the words to say and the peace to say them. When we are filled with the Holy Spirit, we are fitting our feet with the readiness of the Gospel of Peace.*

Have an altar call for those who have not received the baptism of the Holy Spirit and for those who want to be filled again so they have the words to tell others the Gospel.

## Small Group Craft: Shoe Verse

*Supplies needed:* Colorful cardstock (1 for each student), marker, scissors, crayons, stickers, hole punch, ribbons

Trace each child's foot onto the cardstock with a marker. Have each student cut out the foot and write today's memory verse on it.

Luke 12:12 (NIV) For the Holy Spirit will teach you at that time what you should say.

Then allow the students to decorate their cutouts. If you have younger students, they may need extra help with this craft.

Punch holes in each foot and thread a ribbon through them, so the students can hang them in their rooms as a reminder.

## Small Group Optional: Missions Project

This would be a good week to do a missions project with your students.

# Lesson 9 – My Faith in God is My Shield (Shield of Faith)

**Focus Point:** Faith in God protects us from the devil's lies.

**Goal:** Students will learn that when they trust everything God says in faith, any lies the enemy tries to attack them with are destroyed.

**Verse of the Day: Ephesians 6:16 (NIV)** *In addition to all this, take up the shield of faith, with which you can extinguish all the flaming arrows of the evil one.*

**Supplies Needed:**

- *Building a Fortress in God* Downloadable Resources
- Kid James Puppet (optional)
- Army uniform costume for skit (optional)
- wadded up pieces of paper – 1 per student (optional – beanbags or soft balls)
- trash can lids or large pieces of cardboard and duct tape – 1 per student
- 3 tennis balls (optional)
- blindfold
- chair
- shield
- ½ teaspoon, 1 teaspoon, 1 tablespoon measuring spoons
- 4 clear cups
- vinegar
- baking soda
- tray
- soda 2 liter bottle
- package of Mentos
- plastic tablecloth
- posterboard (1 for each student)
- scissors
- glue
- stickers
- crayons
- markers
- paint and brushes (optional)

**Opening:** *Building a Fortress in God Countdown* or *Building a Fortress in God* Slide (Available free with registration of this curriculum.)

**Welcome:** *Welcome to Building a Fortress in God. Today, we're learning about the next piece of armor that God uses to protect us, the shield of faith. In Ephesian 6:16 (NIV), it says, take up the shield of faith, with which you can extinguish all the flaming arrows of the evil one. That's* *pretty awesome. Faith in God can shield us from any lies the devil uses to attack us.*

**Prayer:** Ask a child to pray over the service. Encourage him or her to end the prayer with "In the Name of Jesus. Amen."

**Rules:** (use rules slide) Go over the 5 Ups Rules.

Go over the *5 Ups Rules*: 1. Sit up straight. 2. Listen up. 3. Hush up. 4. Don't get up and run around or go to the bathroom. 5. Worship Up! (stand up and participate during praise and worship)

**Theme or Activity Songs:** Choose one or two fast-moving activity or theme songs that go with the curriculum.

**Game Time: Shield** (use game time slide)

*Supplies Needed:* wadded up pieces of paper – 1 per student (optional – beanbags or soft balls), trash can lids or large pieces of cardboard and duct tape – 1 per student

*Preparation:* If using cardboard, make a handle on the back using duct tape.

Divide students into 2 teams. One team will have shields. The other team will have wadded up pieces of paper. When you say start, the students with the paper balls will throw them and try to tap the students on the other team on the chest. If a student is tapped, he must sit out. The student with the shield who stays in the longest wins. The next round, have students switch whether they have shields or paper balls.

**Memory Verse Skit:** (use *Building a Fortress in God* Lesson 9, slide a and/or Kid James Skit #9 Video)

*Supplies needed:* Kid James Puppet (Optional)

*Kid James:* Howdy, kids. I'm Kid James. I'm a Bible, but not just any Bible. I teach children the Word of God. Today's verse is about our shield of faith. Ephesians 6;16 (NIV) says, "In addition to all this, take up the shield of faith, with which you can extinguish all the flaming arrows of the evil one." We know that the devil is the father of lies. He will try to convince you not to believe or have faith in God or His Word, but we can hold up our faith in God as a shield to stop any flaming arrow of lies the devil throws at us.

**Offering:**

*When you give an offering to God, do you trust Him with your money? Luke 6:38 (NIV) says, "Give, and it will be given to you." We don't have to worry about giving our money to God. We can have faith in Him to take care of us if we give to Him.*

**Skit: Sgt. Do Right Uses His Shield** (optional - use Sgt. Do Right Skit #9 Video)

*Supplies Needed:* Army uniform, trashcan lid, 3 tennis balls (optional)

(Sgt. Do Right marches into the room with a shield and 3 tennis balls and salutes.)

*Leader:* Hello, Sgt. Do Right. What do you have there?

*Sgt. Do Right:* Good morning, Sir (Ma'am). Today, I have my shield of faith. It will block all attacks from the enemy and keep me safe.

*Leader:* Sgt. Do Right, that isn't really a shield. I hate to tell you this, but it's a trash can lid.

*Sgt. Do Right:* Maybe, Sir (Ma'am), but I'm using it as a shield. Let me show you how it works. Take these tennis balls.

*Leader:* Okay. (takes tennis balls)

*Sgt. Do Right:* Now I want you to throw these tennis balls at me as hard as you can.

*Leader:* But tennis balls are hard. I'm afraid I'll hurt you.

*Sgt. Do Right:* It'll be all right, Sir (Ma'am). I have my shield of faith. It will protect me.

*Leader:* If you say so.

(Leader throws the balls. Sgt. Do Right holds up his shield. It protects him from the first ball, but then he drops his shield and yelps as the balls hit him.)

*Sgt. Do Right:* Oww, that hurt. (rubs his arm) I don't understand why it didn't work. I read how the shield of faith would protect me. Maybe the shield of faith doesn't work after all.

*Leader:* The shield of faith works, but you weren't using the shield of faith to protect you. You were using a trash can lid.

*Sgt. Do Right:* But that's all I have. Where do I get the shield of faith? Do you think they might have one in the Army surplus store?

*Leader:* This isn't a shield you can get at any store. It's an invisible shield. When you have faith and trust in God's Word and in Jesus Christ, your faith operates as a shield to protect you against anything the enemy throws at you.

*Sgt. Do Right:* I don't understand.

*Leader:* I'll give you an example. Have you ever done anything wrong and asked God to forgive you?

*Sgt. Do Right:* Yes, once when my captain chewed me out, I was angry and yelled at one of my friends. He didn't do anything wrong, but I still yelled at him. I asked God to forgive me, and I asked my friend to forgive me. Both God and my friend forgave me.

*Leader:* So, if the devil reminded you of the way you treated your friend, what would you do?

*Sgt. Do Right:* I would know that isn't true because 1 John 1:9 (ICB) says, "But if we confess our sins, he will forgive our sins. We can trust God. He does what is right. He will make us clean from all the wrongs we have done."

*Leader:* Do you know what you did just then? You used your shield of faith. When we have faith in God and what He says in His Word, we are using the shield of faith. That faith will protect us from the lies of the enemy.

*Sgt. Do Right:* That's amazing. So I had the shield of faith all along and didn't even know it. I'm going to tell my fellow soldiers about how to get the shield of faith. I have to go now. Bye.

(Salutes and exits)

**Verse of the Day: Ephesian 6:16 (NIV)** *In addition to all this, take up the shield of faith, with which you can extinguish all the flaming arrows of the evil one.*

**Memory Verse Talk:** (use *Building a Fortress in God* Lesson 9, slide a)

Have your students repeat the verse a couple of times.

*Have you ever seen the devil throw fiery darts at someone? I haven't either. Instead, the devil tries to destroy our faith in God by throwing lies at us to try to get us to doubt God and His Word. Have you ever thought, "God doesn't really care about me," or "God will never forgive me for this"? Those are the fiery darts the devil throws at us. If he can get us to doubt God's love and forgiveness, he will convince us that what God says about us isn't true. We need to hold up our faith in God when those lies invade our thoughts.*

**Memory Verse Activity: Stand if…** (use *Building a Fortress in God* Lesson 9, slide a)

Have students stand and say the memory verse if any of the statements you say relate to them. Here are a few statements you can use.

Stand and say the verse if…

You have brown hair.

You're wearing something blue.

You brushed your teeth today.

You took a bath or shower today.

You went to school this week.

End with "stand and say the verse if you love Jesus."

## Bible Story: A Roman Centurion Has Faith

(Matthew 8:5-13)

*In Hebrews 11:1 (ICB), the Bible tells us what faith is. It says, "Faith means being sure of the things we hope for. And faith means knowing that something is real even if we do not see it."*

*I'm going to tell you a true story about a man Jesus had a conversation with, and I want you to listen carefully and tell me if you think this man had faith.*

*The man was a Roman centurion. He was a soldier in charge of a hundred men. The Jews didn't like the Romans because many of the soldiers were harsh and unfair to them, but this man was different. He heard about Jesus healing people and believed them.*

*One day, the centurion's servant became very sick. He knew Jesus healed a lot of people, so he traveled to where Jesus was and asked Him to heal his servant. Jesus offered to go with him and heal the servant.*

*But in Matthew 9:8-9 (NIV), "The centurion replied, 'Lord, I do not deserve to have you come under my roof. But just say the word, and my servant will be healed. For I myself am a man under authority, with soldiers under me. I tell this one, "Go," and he goes; and that one, "Come," and he comes. I say to my servant, "Do this," and he does it.'"*

*In other words, the centurion had so much faith, he didn't need Jesus to come heal his servant. He believed that if Jesus said the man was healed, he was healed.*

*Do we believe the centurion had faith?* Allow students to answer.

*So what happened next? The Bible says Jesus was amazed at the centurion's faith. He told the centurion his servant was healed. When the centurion got home, his servant had been healed at the very moment Jesus spoke.*

*Wow. I'd love to have faith that amazes Jesus. Wouldn't you?*

**Praise and Worship:** Choose a couple of fast songs and a slow song to lead children into praise and worship. You can have a children's praise team, but until they understand leading praise and worship, have an adult leader or you be the worship leader.

## Object Lessons:

**1. Object Lesson: Trust** (use *Building a Fortress in God* Lesson 9, slide b)

Supplies Needed: blindfold, chair

Show slide b. *Charles Blondin was a tightrope walker in the 1800s. He was famous because he stretched a rope across Niagara Falls and performed on the tightrope. He would carry all sorts of things while walking across. One time, he walked across on stilts. Another time, he was blindfolded. He even cooked an omelet and ate it halfway across the rope. At the end of his act, he would take a wheelbarrow across, then he would ask someone to ride in the wheelbarrow. It was one thing to believe Blondin could take a person across a tightrope in a wheelbarrow, but it takes faith to get into that wheelbarrow.*

*So do you trust me?* Choose two students to assist you, preferrably students who say they trust you.

Stand behind the first student. Tell the student to fall back. Assure him you will catch him. Make sure to pay attention. When the student falls, catch him.

Blindfold the second student. Give her instructions such as walk two spaces, turn to the right, etc. Direct her until she's standing directly in front of a chair. Instruct her to sit down without feeling to see if something's there.

*There's a big difference between believing God and having trust and faith in Him. These students didn't just believe me. They trusted me. When we use the shield of faith, we don't just believe in God, we trust and have faith in Him to do what He says and to protect us. We obey Him even if we don't understand what He is planning.*

**2. Object Lesson: Different Kinds of Shields** (use *Building a Fortress in God* Lesson 9, slides c-g)

*Supplies needed:* shield (Can purchase online or at a Bible bookstore)

Show slide c. *A buckler shield was popular in the Middle Ages. Warriors would carry long swords, and the buckler was small and easy to carry. The warrior could carry a sword and a shield. But it didn't protect very much of the body. The warrior would have to hold it in the place that was being attacked, or he would be killed. If more than one enemy was attacking, he was through.*

Show slide d. *There were other types of shields in the Middle Ages, the round shield, the kite shield. These were very heavy and still didn't protect the whole body, but they were bigger than buckler shields. The warriors had to lift their shields when they were attacked, but the shields were so heavy, they couldn't protect themselves with a shield and fight at the same time.*

Show slide e. *Then there are shields that policemen use. They're called ballistic shields. When SWAT police have to make a dangerous raid where the bad guys have guns, they use these shields. These shields usually cover the whole body and head but have a place where police can see out. Of course, if the bad guy shoots their eyes, the shield won't protect them.*

Show slide f. Optional – Show this YouTube video clip. (https://youtu.be/q23jpbSu3dQ?si=6itsYW-8qLBvTQt1) *This is Captain America's shield.*

*It's round and resists fire and bullets. It can even be used as a weapon. But it's still small. Like the buckler shield, it has to be placed in the exact spot the enemy is attacking or it's useless.*

Show slide g. *This is the shield Roman soldiers carried during Bible times. It's called a scutum. It was light enough to hold easily, and it protected the whole body. Soldiers could also use it to attack the enemy by pushing the enemy back. The only problem is it wasn't very strong. Sometimes a sword or hatchet would break it in pieces.*

*The only shield that is completely reliable is the shield of faith. It is invisible and doesn't weigh anything, so we can carry it everywhere we go. It protects us in every way from any attacks of the enemy.*

*For instance, if the enemy tells us we're all alone, we can have faith in God's Word in Hebrews 13:5 (NIV), where God said, "Never will I leave you; never will I forsake you."*

*When we're afraid and in trouble and don't know what to do, we can trust Isaiah 41:13 (NIV). "For I am the LORD your God who takes hold of your right hand and says to you, Do not fear; I will help you."*

*When we take up our shields of faith, we know God will protect us from anything the enemy throws at us.*

## Message: Measuring Your Faith

*Supplies Needed:* shield, ½ teaspoon, 1 teaspoon, 1 tablespoon measuring spoon, 4 clear cups, vinegar, baking soda, tray, Soda 2 liter bottle, package of Mentos, plastic tablecloth

*Preparation:* Label cups by numbers 1 – 4. Cup #1 - Pour a small amount of vinegar in the cup and fill with water until it is half full; Cup #2 – Pour a little more vinegar and fill with water until half full; Cup #3 – Pour half vinegar and half water until the cup is full; Cup # 4 – fill cup half full with vinegar. Place cups on tray to catch any overflow. Place the open bottle of soda and a package of Mentos on the tablecloth.

Show shield. *When we are saved, God gives each one of us a shield of faith. It's a small shield and not very strong, but we each have one. Did you know we can grow our faith until our shield is huge and strong? Here's how.*

*In Romans 12:3, the Bible says that God has given us a measure of faith. When you give your life to Jesus, you're given a small measure of faith. Let's measure out that faith.* Place ½ teaspoon of baking soda into cup #1. *As you can see, there is a small reaction. When bad things happen and we pray, we know God is with us.*

*You can continue to strengthen your shield of faith by learning and memorizing more about God and His promises through His Word, the Bible. For instance, Jeremiah 29:11 (NIV) says, "'For I know the plans I have for you,' declares the Lord, 'plans to prosper you and not to harm you, plans to give you hope and a future.'"* Measure 1 teaspoon of baking soda into cup #2. *As you memorize God's Word and believe His promise, your faith has a greater reaction. Your shield of faith is stronger now.*

*You can also strengthen your faith by obeying God even when it's hard. In Hebrews 11:7 (NLT), it says, "It was by faith that Noah built a large boat to save his family from the flood. He obeyed God, who warned him about things that had never happened before. By his faith Noah condemned the rest of the world, and he received the righteousness that comes by faith." Noah grew his faith when he obeyed God even though he'd never seen rain, let alone a flood. You can strengthen your faith by obeying God when He impresses upon your spirit to do something. He might want you to tell your best friend how to be saved. Or He might want you to sit with the unpopular kid at school. He might even have you do something weird that you don't understand.*

Tell a story about when you obeyed God even though you didn't understand why He wanted you to do something. Measure 1 tablespoon into cup #3. *As you can see, the kind of faith that obeys God is powerful.*

*The next way you can strengthen your faith is by praying God-sized prayers. In Matthew 7:20 (NIV) Jesus said, "Truly I tell you, if you have faith as small as a mustard seed, you can say to this mountain, 'Move from here to there,' and it will move. Nothing will be impossible for you."*

*These kinds of prayers are the kind you pray to heal the sick or to restore your parents' marriages, or to deliver someone from a dangerous situation. Don't be discouraged if sometimes God doesn't answer these prayers right away or in the way you want. As you continue to believe and pray God-sized prayers, your prayers will be answered. That will strengthen your faith for more God-sized prayers.* Pour 2 tablespoons of baking soda into cup #4.

*The next kind of faith you can't do anything to make stronger. It is the gift of faith. Sometimes God will give you a gift of faith to believe the impossible. It isn't something you can create by the things you do or pray. It's a kind of faith God gives at the times He decides. This kind of faith can heal cancer or raise people from the dead. It is an amazing gift from God, and it is explosive faith.* Pour the Mentos into the soda.

For response time, ask if any students need prayer to help them strengthen their faith or if they need a God-sized miracle. Have your students anoint and pray for each other. Show them where to lay their hands during prayer. Help them pray by laying your hand on their backs while they are praying.

## Small Group Craft: Shields

*Supplies needed:* Posterboard (1 for each student), scissors glue, stickers, crayons, markers, paint and brushes (optional)

*Preparation:* Cut out shield on poster board. Examples of different shape shields are in the picture below. Cut strips of posterboard and glue them on the back of each shield to make a handle.

# Lesson 10 – My God Makes Me Brave (Helmet of Salvation)

**Focus Point:** Because God is mighty, I don't need to be afraid.

**Goal:** Students will learn that God is on their side, so they don't have to worry or fear any danger.

**Verse of the Day: Psalm 46:1-2 (NIV)** *God is our refuge and strength, an ever-present help in trouble. Therefore we will not fear, though the earth give way and the mountains fall into the heart of the sea,*

**Supplies Needed:**

- *Building a Fortress in God* Downloadable Resources
- Kid James Puppet (optional)
- Army uniform costume for skit (optional)
- bed sheets (1 sheet per 6 students)
- army, football, or knight's helmet, or metal pot large enough to wear on your head
- hammer
- 2 bags of chips
- hair dryer
- ping-pong ball

**Opening**: *Building a Fortress in God Countdown* or *Building a Fortress in God* Slide (Available free with registration of this curriculum.)

**Welcome:** *Welcome to Building a Fortress in God. God is mighty, mightier than anything in the universe. He created the universe. He also loves His children, those who have accepted Him as their Savior. If you are a child of God, there is never any reason to be afraid. That doesn't mean you won't feel the emotion of fear. That's normal. But it does mean you can trust God to be a present help in time of trouble. God is mightier than anything you fear.*

**Prayer:** Ask a child to pray over the service. Encourage him or her to end the prayer with "In the Name of Jesus. Amen."

**Rules:** (use rules slide) Go over the 5 Ups Rules.

Go over the *5 Ups Rules*: 1. Sit up straight. 2. Listen up. 3. Hush up. 4. Don't get up and run around or go to the bathroom. 5. Worship Up! (stand up and participate during praise and worship)

**Theme or Activity Songs:** Choose one or two fast-moving activity or theme songs that go with the curriculum.

### Game Time: Fish Race (use game time slide)

*Supplies Needed:* bed sheets (1 sheet per 6 students)

Divide students into teams of six. Each team will wrap one sheet around all of them. The teams are schools of fish. The teams will race to the finish line, but they have to work together and stay wrapped in their sheets. The team that gets to the finish line first wins.

*You all had to work or swim with your teammates to race to the finish line. Fish swim in teams called schools to keep them safe from larger fish and sharks. But God is all the safety we need. He will keep us safe if we belong to Him. We don't have to fear the big fish or sharks in our world because God is mightier than all of them.*

### Memory Verse Skit: (use *Building a Fortress in God* Lesson 10, slide a and/or Kid James Skit #10 Video)

*Supplies needed:* Kid James Puppet (optional)

*Kid James:* Howdy, kids. I'm Kid James. I'm a Bible, but not just any Bible. I teach children the Word of God. Today's verse is about how God is so mighty that we don't have to be afraid. We can be brave because He keeps us safe. Psalm 46:1-2 (NIV) says, "God is our refuge and strength, an ever-present help in trouble. Therefore we will not fear, though the earth give way and the mountains fall into the heart of the sea."

## Offering:

*When you give in the offering, it is powerful. God blesses your offering and every other offering together to help others in a way that you alone couldn't help. God will make our offering more powerful than anything we could give, and He will use them in mighty ways.*

### Skit: Sgt. Do Right Talks About the Helmet of Salvation (optional - use Sgt. Do Right Skit #10 Video)

*Supplies Needed:* Army uniform (optional)

(Sgt. Do Right marches into the room and salutes.)

*Leader:* Hello, Sgt. Do Right.

*Sgt. Do Right:* Sgt. Do Right reporting as ordered, Sir (Ma'am).

*Leader:* So how did things go last week with your captain? Did you get the Jeep fixed?

*Sgt. Do Right:* I didn't get it fixed, Sir (Ma'am). So I marched up to the captain, saluted, and told him I couldn't fix it.

*Leader:* That was so brave. What did the captain say?

*Sgt. Do Right:* He said he wasn't sure anyone could fix that Jeep, but he wanted me to try. He wasn't angry about it at all.

*Leader:* That's great, Sergeant. I know you were worried about telling him. How did you get the courage to do it?

*Sgt. Do Right:* After I talked to you last week, I started thinking how God is mighty. I thought about how He was mighty enough to save me from my sins, so He would be mighty enough to help me even if I was afraid.

*Leader:* It sounds like you put on your helmet of salvation.

*Sgt. Do Right:* My helmet of salvation?

*Leader:* That's right. The helmet of salvation is one of the pieces of the armor of God.

*Sgt. Do Right:* A helmet is very important when you go into battle. It protects your head.

*Leader:* It's important in spiritual battles too. When Jesus saves you from your sins, He becomes your helmet of salvation. Even when you're afraid, you can be brave because you know God is mightier than anything you're afraid of.

*Sgt. Do Right:* I'm glad I have the helmet of salvation.

*Leader:* Me too. I wouldn't want to go through life without God's protection.

*Sgt. Do Right:* I wouldn't either.

(Salutes and exits)

**Verse of the Day: Psalm 46:1-2 (NIV)** *God is our refuge and strength, an ever-present help in trouble. Therefore we will not fear, though the earth give way and the mountains fall into the heart of the sea.*

**Memory Verse Talk:** (use *Building a Fortress in God* Lesson 10, slide a)

Have your students repeat the verse a couple of times.

*Everybody is afraid sometimes. Fear is an emotion that keeps us from doing foolish things. What are some things you're afraid of?* Allow students to answer.

*This verse talks about a mountain falling into the sea. How many of you would be afraid of that?* Allow students to answer.

*When God is our refuge and strength, He is stronger than any trouble we face. When we realize how mighty God is, even if we are afraid, we can be brave, even if a mountain falls down beside us.*

**Memory Verse Activity: Circle Verse** (use *Building a Fortress in God* Lesson 10, slide a)

Have the students stand in a circle. You start the Circle Verse by saying the verse address. The first student in the circle says the first word of the verse. The second child in the circle says the second word, etc. To make it more competitive, you can have any student who says the wrong word leave the circle, or you can just allow the next student to say the correct word.

**Bible Story: 3 Young Men Are Brave Because God is Mighty**

(Daniel 3)

Instruct your students that when they hear these words during this story, they should respond loudly in the following ways:

Shadrach, Meshach, and Abednego – cheer loudly

Worship Idols – We only worship God

King Nebuchadnezzar – Boo, boo

Fiery Furnace – Wow, that's hot

Jesus or God – God is mighty to save

Rehearse these words with your students a few times, then tell the story.

*Along time ago, there were three young men who had been captured by King Nebuchadnezzar (boo) and sent to live in a land called Babylon. The three teenagers were named Shadrach, Meshach, and Abednego (cheer loudly). These teenagers were taken away from everyone they knew and were forced to live in King Nebuchadnezzar's (boo) court to serve him. I'm sure they were afraid and lonely sometimes, but they knew God (God is mighty to save) was mightier than all their fears. They knew God (God is mighty to save) would help them.*

*One day, King Nebuchadnezzar (boo) built a large statue of himself in the middle of the city. He ordered everyone to bow down and worship the statue every time music played. Anyone who didn't bow down would be thrown into a fiery furnace (Wow, that's hot). The king had a big ego problem.*

*Our three young heroes, Shadrach, Meshach, and Abednego (cheer loudly), heard the order, but they decided that if the music played while they were in the center of town, they would not bow down. They knew God commands us only to worship Him, so they weren't going to worship King Nebuchadnezzar (boo).*

*Shadrach, Meshach, and Abednego (cheer loudly) were probably feeling a little afraid. Wouldn't you be? I mean a gigantic furnace with fire in it. I burned my finger a few times, and it hurt. They would be burned to a crisp in that fiery furnace (Wow, that's hot). But they knew God (God* is mighty to save) *is our refuge and strength, an ever-present help in trouble. They knew God* (God is mighty to save) *could deliver them, and so they were brave even when they felt afraid.*

*The day finally came. Shadrach, Meshach, and Abednego* (cheer loudly) *were in the center of town near the statue when the music began to play. Everyone around them bowed to the ground and worshipped the statue. There were probably some other Israelites who bowed down and thought it was okay as long as they didn't worship the statue in their hearts. But these three young men stood tall and refused to bow.*

*When King Nebuchadnezzar* (boo) *heard the three teenagers refused to bow when the music played, he was furious. The king ordered his guards to bring them to him. When Shadrach, Meshach, and Abednego* (cheer loudly) *arrived, King Nebuchadnezzar* (boo) *told them what he'd heard. He would give them one more chance. He would have his musicians play music, and if the three brave Israelites bowed down, everything would be fine. But if they didn't, they would be thrown into the fiery furnace* (Wow, that's hot).

*Do you think Shadrach, Meshach, and Abednego* (cheer loudly) *were scared?* Allow students to answer. *I would be scared. Wouldn't you?* Allow students to answer. *Remember though, fear is an emotion. There's nothing wrong with being afraid. When Scripture tells us not to be afraid, it means trust God* (God is mighty to save), *and don't give in to that emotion of fear. That's what being brave is.*

*In Daniel 3:16-18 (NIV), Shadrach, Meshach, and Abednego* (cheer loudly) *answered the king.* "*O Nebuchadnezzar* (boo), *we have no need to answer you in this matter. If this be so, our God* (God is mighty to save) *whom we serve is able to deliver us from the burning fiery furnace* (Wow, that's hot), *and he will deliver us out of your hand, O king. But if not, be it known to you, O king, that we will not serve your gods or worship the golden image that you have set up.*"

*Wow, that was brave. Think about what these three brave men said. They said, "We know God* (God is mighty to save) *is able to deliver us. We know God* (God is mighty to save) *will deliver us. And even if He doesn't, we still won't bow. When you know God* (God is mighty to save) *is mightier than any trouble you face, and you know He loves you because you asked Him to be Lord* (God is mighty to save) *of your life and to save you, you can be brave even when you're afraid.*

*The king was so angry, he ordered the heat to be turned up seven times hotter. Then he ordered his guards to throw Shadrach, Meshach, and Abednego* (cheer loudly) *into the fiery furnace* (Wow, that's hot). *It was so hot that the guards throwing them in caught on fire and burned up.*

*Then something amazing happened. The fire burned off the ropes tying the three teenagers' hands together, but they didn't catch on fire. Then a fourth man appeared in the fire. The king was also amazed. He said he saw them walking around in the fire, and the fourth man looked like the Son of God* (God is mighty to save). *Think about that for a moment. Jesus* (God is mighty to save), *years before He came to Earth as a baby, went into that fire to save Shadrach, Meshach, and Abednego* (cheer loudly).

*The king told the three teenagers to come out of the fire. When they did, they didn't even smell like smoke, and their clothes and hair weren't even singed. The king and his men were astonished. The king ordered that anybody who spoke against the God* (God is mighty to save) *of Shadrach, Meshach, and Abednego* (cheer loudly) *would be destroyed. And he promoted the brave heroes.*

**Praise and Worship:** Choose a couple of fast songs and a slow song to lead children into praise and worship. You can have a children's praise team, but until they understand leading praise and worship, have an adult leader or you be the worship leader.

## Object Lessons:

### 1. Object Lesson: Helmet of Salvation

Supplies Needed: army, football helmet, knight's helmet, or metal pot, and hammer, 2 bags of chips

Put the helmet on. *Why do football players and soldiers wear helmets?* Allow students to answer. If none of the students say to protect their heads, suggest that answer. *Let me show you an example.*

Lay a bag of chips on the table. Smash the bag of chips with the hammer. *Without a helmet, a soldier or football player might get their head smashed in like this bag of chips was. But with the helmet...* Set the second bag of chips under the helmet. Hit it several times with the hammer. Open the bag of chips and eat a couple. *The helmet protected the bag of chips just as it protects the head of a football player in a game or a solder in battle.*

*God has given us invisible armor called the armor of God. One piece of armor is the helmet of salvation. Many of you are already wearing the helmet of salvation. When you give your life to Jesus and ask Him to be your Lord and Savior, He saves you and gives you the helmet of salvation. The helmet of salvation will change the way you think about things. When bad things happen, and the emotion of fear rises up, we can stand in the goodness of God because we know,* point to head, *God is our ever-present help in time of trouble, and He loves us. We are His. Not only that, but He is mightier than any problem we face. Because we have on the helmet of salvation, we can trust in God to protect and deliver us.*

### 2. Object Lesson: God Gives Us Power to Trust Him

*Supplies needed:* hair dryer, ping-pong ball

*God is mighty, mightier than any trouble we face, but did you know He gives us power to trust Him in times of trouble, even when we're afraid?*

Hold the ping-pong ball in the air and drop it several times while saying the following. *Sometimes we're like this ping-pong ball. When trouble comes, we want to trust God, but we feel too afraid. We just can't rise above our fear.*

Place the ping-pong ball on the hair dryer and turn it on while saying the following. *We can't overcome our fear and trust God on our own. We need the power of God to help us. He is mighty, and He loves us. When we ask Him to give us the power to trust Him in times of trouble, He will do it. Just as the air holds this ping-pong ball up, we can rise above our troubles when we rely on God to help us.*

## Message: God Can Make You Brave

*Supplies Needed:* Helmet

*When you are afraid and need help, I want you to remember these five things.*

*First, wear your helmet.* Put on the helmet. *If you have asked Jesus into your lives and made Him your Lord and Savior, you are saved from your sins and are wearing the invisible helmet of salvation. If you aren't saved, in a moment, we'll give you an opportunity to accept Jesus Christ as your Lord and Savior and give your life to Him.*

*Second, remember how mighty God is. He is mightier than any fear or problem you have.*

*Third, remember God loves you. He is there for you. He will help you through any trouble you face.*

*Fourth, we can trust God to help us. If you are afraid, you can ask God to help you and still trust Him. He can make you brave even when you're afraid.*

*Fifth, if God leads you to do something, trust Him enough to do it even if you have to do it afraid. He will give the courage you need to be brave.*

For response time, ask if any students need to be saved or if they need God to help them with their fears. Anoint and pray for them. During worship time, anoint and pray for every student to trust God to help them.

## Small Group Discussion: Talk About Fears

Tell your students a story about when you were afraid and God helped you be brave. Emphasize that you were still afraid, but you trusted God. Also talk about missionaries overseas who face fearful situations and how God helps them. If your church doesn't support a missionary in this situation, you can find stories about missionaries at Every Home for Christ (https://everyhome.org/) or at Kids in Courage (https://www.persecution.com/kids/).

# Lesson 11 – Basic Training in God's Word (Sword of the Spirit)

**Focus Point:** I can use God's Word to fight the enemy.

**Goal:** Students will learn that the Bible is one of the greatest enemies we have against the devil, but we must learn to use the Word of God for it to be effective

**Verse of the Day: Hebrews 4:12 (NIrV)** *The word of God is alive and active. It is sharper than any sword that has two edges. It cuts deep enough to separate soul from spirit. It can separate bones from joints. It judges the thoughts and purposes of the heart.*

**Supplies Needed:**

- *Building a Fortress in God* Downloadable Resources
- Kid James Puppet (optional)
- Army uniform costume for skit (optional)
- The Bible
- 4 pool noodles
- 2 jump ropes
- various obstacles
- clear glass
- spoon
- Red Bull
- chocolate milk
- baby bottle with milk
- jar of baby food
- beef jerky
- sword (can be play, prop, or real)
- tools
- mirror

**Opening**: *Building a Fortress in God Countdown* or *Building a Fortress in God* Slide (Available free with registration of this curriculum.)

**Welcome:** *Welcome to Building a Fortress in God. Today, we're going to learn about one of the greatest weapons we have to use against the devil. Can you guess what it is?* Allow students to answer. Show Bible. *It's the God's Word, also called the Sword of the Spirit.*

**Prayer:** Ask a child to pray over the service. Encourage him or her to end the prayer with "In the Name of Jesus. Amen."

**Rules:** (use rules slide) Go over the 5 Ups Rules.

Go over the *5 Ups Rules*: 1. Sit up straight. 2. Listen up. 3. Hush up. 4. Don't get up and run around or go to the bathroom. 5. Worship Up! (stand up and participate during praise and worship)

**Theme or Activity Songs:** Choose one or two fast-moving activity or theme songs that go with the curriculum.

**Game Time: Soldier Training** (use game time slide)

*Supplies Needed:* 4 pool noodles, 2 jump ropes, obstacles

*Preparation:* Set up obstacles on either side of the room. Make sure each side of the room has the same obstacles. Use the pool noodles for students to jump over. If some students are young and don't know how to jump rope, have them hold the jump ropes and jump over them.

Divide students into two equal teams. If you have an odd number of students, choose one student to stand in the front and say go.

*Soldiers don't automatically know how to march, salute, and go into battle when they first join the army. They have to train for battle in something called Basic Training. We're going to do a little basic training now by running this obstacle course.*

Show students how to run the obstacle course, then have a relay race. First team to finish wins.

**Memory Verse Skit:** (use *Building a Fortress in God* Lesson 11, slide a and/or Kid James Skit #11 Video)

*Supplies needed:* Kid James Puppet (optional)

*Kid James:* Howdy, kids. I'm Kid James. I'm a Bible, but not just any Bible. I teach children the Word of God. Today's verse is about the Word of God. When we learn to use it effectively, it is one of our greatest weapons against the devil. Hebrews 4:12 (NIrV) says, "The word of God is alive and active. It is sharper than any sword that has two edges. It cuts deep enough to separate soul from spirit. It can separate bones from joints. It judges the thoughts and purposes of the heart." The Word of God is anything God says. Many of the words of God are contained in the Bible. That's why the Bible is called the Word of God. It can even separate the soul from the spirit. That means it can determine if what you think God is telling you is your own thoughts or God's Word. It can even reveal if your thoughts and plans are right with God or not. The Bible is an important weapon to use against our enemy, the devil.

## Offering:

*God's Word talks a lot about how we should give in the offering. 2 Corinthians 9:7 (NIV) says, "Each of you should give what you have decided in your heart to give, not reluctantly or under compulsion, for God loves a cheerful giver." While we're giving today, let us give cheerfully. Why don't we start now by cheering?* Encourage students to clap and cheer.

**Skit: Sgt. Do Right and Weapons Training** (optional - use Sgt. Do Right Skit #11 Video)

*Supplies Needed:* Army uniform (optional)

(Sgt. Do Right marches into the room and salutes.)

*Leader:* Hello, Sgt. Do Right.

*Sgt. Do Right:* Sgt. Do Right reporting, Sir (Ma'am).

*Leader:* I thought you would be in weapons training today. How come you're here instead?

*Sgt. Do Right:* I don't need weapons training, so I decided to skip it.

*Leader:* But Sgt. Do Right, how can you learn to fire a rifle if you don't go to weapons training?

*Sgt. Do Right:* Nothing to it. I'll just pull the trigger and pow, it will fire.

*Leader:* It will fire all right, but it might not shoot at what you're aiming at. It might hurt an innocent person.

*Sgt. Do Right:* I never thought of that. I just assumed wherever I point it, it will fire.

*Leader:* Not exactly. There's a lot more to it. For instance, if you don't stand and hold the gun correctly, you might get hurt.

*Sgt. Do Right:* (shakes his head) I don't see how I could get hurt just by pulling a trigger.

*Leader:* If you don't hold the butt on your shoulder right, the kick back from the rifle could hit you in the face or knock you down. Weapons training is important even in spiritual warfare.

*Sgt. Do Right:* How could it help in spiritual warfare?

*Leader:* God's Word is called the Sword of the Spirit, but if we have never read it or learned about it, it won't help us. We'll be vulnerable to the lies of the enemy.

*Sgt. Do Right:* I have to go now.

*Leader:* Where are you going?

*Sgt. Do Right:* I'm going to weapons training. I need to learn how to use my weapon. Bye.

(Salutes and exits)

**Verse of the Day: Hebrews 4:12 (NIrV)** *The word of God is alive and active. It is sharper than any sword that has two edges. It cuts deep enough to separate soul from spirit. It can separate bones from joints. It judges the thoughts and purposes of the heart.*

**Memory Verse Talk:** (use *Building a Fortress in God* Lesson 11, slide a)

Have your students repeat the verse a couple of times.

*Did you know memorizing is a great way to keep your brain active and alert? Memorizing key verses in the Word of God not only keeps your brain active and alert, it keeps your spirit active and alert. It's a great way to learn how to use the Word of God. That's why we always have a memory verse every week.*

If you have prizes for memorizing weekly verses, this might be a great week to remind students of the prizes they could win. If not, this week would be a great time to start. You could have a chart with the students' names where they get stickers when they memorize the verses, and you could have some type of prize each week or a grand prize each quarter. If you use the handout family devotions sheets each week, you could also give prizes for reading all of the verses.

It's also a great idea to start a church store with kids' bucks. You can give out kids' bucks for memorizing verses and doing the weekly devotion sheets and have a store where they can buy items with their kids' bucks.

Weekly devotion sheets and a kids' bucks template can be found in *Building a Fortress in God* downloadable resources.

### Memory Verse Activity: Sing it Out (use *Building a Fortress in God* Lesson 11, slide a)

Divide students into teams. Give these teams five to ten minutes to come up with a rap song for today's memory verse. They can also set the verse to music for another song. Make sure to include a couple of older students or musical students with each team. If you have younger students, you could have an adult or teen helper on each team. Allow the teams to sing the verse in front of everyone.

### Object Lesson: The Bible Separates Us from Sin Part 1

*Supplies needed:* clear glass, spoon, Red Bull, chocolate milk

*When we study God's Word and apply it to our lives, it becomes alive and active within us. The chocolate milk represents us before we were saved.* Pour chocolate milk in glass.

*The Red Bull represents the Word of God living in us. The more we read and study the Word of God, the more it will affect our lives.* Pour in Red Bull. Make sure the mixture is half and half.

*We'll come back to this later and see what happens.*

### Bible Story: Timothy Gets Spiritual Training

(1 & 2 Timothy)

*Today, we're going to learn how a young man in the Bible got his spiritual training. Timothy was born in Lystra. His father was a Greek, and his mother, Eunice, was a devout Jew. He also had a grandmother named Lois who loved the Lord. Timothy loved God, and he loved God's Word. He*

*especially loved reading about how the Messiah would come. He and his family didn't know Jesus had already come to Earth. They didn't have social media back then, so they hadn't heard the news yet.*

*One day, Paul came to where they were living and told them the Messiah, Jesus, had come. Timothy and his family were excited. Paul was impressed that Timothy knew the Scriptures so well and invited him to go on missionary journeys with him and Silas. While on these journeys, Timothy learned more about Jesus and about God's Word. Paul was his mentor. Sometimes a spiritual mentor is called a spiritual father or mother, so Paul called Timothy his spiritual son.*

*Although Timothy was young, Paul made him the pastor at the church of Ephesus. He told him not to worry about people thinking he was too young. He was spiritually mature.*

*While Timothy was pastor, Paul wrote him two letters. Some of the things Paul advised him are found in these letters. One of the main things he told Timothy was to continue to study God's Word and to teach it to others. He warned against people who tried to teach false things about God's Word.*

*In 2 Timothy 3:14-17 (NIV) Paul wrote, "But as for you, continue in what you have learned and have become convinced of, because you know those from whom you learned it, and how from infancy you have known the Holy Scriptures, which are able to make you wise for salvation through faith in Christ Jesus. All Scripture is God-breathed and is useful for teaching, rebuking, correcting and training in righteousness, so that the servant of God may be thoroughly equipped for every good work."*

*If Timothy could learn Scripture at an early age and teach it to others, you can too.*

**Praise and Worship:** Choose a couple of fast songs and a slow song to lead children into praise and worship. You can have a children's praise team, but until they understand leading praise and worship, have an adult leader or you be the worship leader.

## Object Lessons:

### 1. Object Lesson: Grow Up

*Supplies Needed:* baby bottle with milk, jar of baby food, beef jerky

*Did you know that you can be spiritually grown up even though you're a child? And adults can be spiritual babies even though they might be adults who have been saved a long time. One way to grow up spiritually is to learn how to use the Word of God.*

Show bottle of milk. *When we're babies, we drink milk from a bottle or our mom's milk. This milk has all the nourishment we need as babies,*

*Spiritual babies need milk too. The Bible says God's Word is like milk for a baby. In 1 Peter 2:2 (NIV), God's Word says, " Like newborn babies, crave pure spiritual milk, so that by it*

*you may grow up in your salvation."*

*This is like someone who doesn't know much about the Bible and has never read it. That person wouldn't start in a book like Leviticus using the King James Version of the Bible. He might start in the Book of Mark or Luke and learn more about who Jesus is, and he'd read in an easy-to-read version like the New International Version or the International Children's Bible. If you don't know how to read yet, you could start with YouVersion Kids and have it read the book of Mark to you, or you could have a parent or older brother or sister read it to you.*

Show baby food. *After a while, a baby needs more than milk, but he isn't ready for grown-up food yet. That's when he starts eating baby food. When we start reading the Bible, eventually we'll start wanting to learn more than just the basics. That's when we start studying the Bible. We find out more of what it says, not just the stories. We start reading more books in the New Testament like Ephesians and Philippians, and we read in Genesis how God created everything or the poetry in Psalms. We start learning more about the people in the Bible like Noah, or Peter, or Paul, or Timothy. We might start using simple Bible studies like on YouVersion Kids or we might study our weekly family devotions sheet we get from children's church. This is the time we might get serious about memorizing Scripture verses and figuring out what those verses are saying to us.*

*But how many of you still drink milk from a bottle or eat baby food?* Allow students to answer. *Milk and baby food are great for babies, but if we want to grow up, we need to eat something more.*

Show beef jerky. *We need meat and vegetables and fruit to become healthy children and adults.*

*Hebrews 5:14 (NIV) says, "But solid food is for the mature, who by constant use have trained themselves to distinguish good from evil."*

*There are some people who don't know what is good and what is evil because they haven't eaten the solid food in the Word of God. If they have read the Bible, they don't believe what it says, or they don't do what it says. They are spiritual babies no matter how old they are.*

Depending on your students, you may want to give some examples such as people who say they are Christians but think it's all right to change their gender or to cuss or to get drunk.

*When we study the meat or solid food of Scripture, we will see what the verses around that verse say. We will find out what the people of that culture were like, so we understand what they're saying. We'll see what the Scripture said to the people then, and we'll pray and ask the Holy Spirit to show us what the Scripture is telling us today. We become spiritual adults no matter what our age is.*

*Now, who would like to take this beef jerky home?* Choose a student who raises his hand.

**2. Object Lesson: The Bible Separates Us From Sin Part 2**

*Supplies needed:* clear glass, spoon, Red Bull, chocolate milk

Hold up the glass. *As you can see, the Red Bull separated from the chocolate milk. The more we read and study God's Word, the more the words of God will become like a sword separating us from the things in our lives that can harm us.*

## Message: Spiritual Training in God's Word

*Supplies Needed:* sword, Bible, tools, mirror

Show sword. *This sword is a powerful weapon, but if I've never learned to sword fight, how do you think I would do using it against an expert sword fighter?* Show some moves. *Probably not too well. If it wasn't a pretend fight, I'd probably get hurt or killed.*

Show Bible. *This Bible is a powerful weapon also, but I need to learn how to use it before I can fight with it against the devil and the power of darkness. As you can see, this Bible is well used. The pages are worn, and it has a lot of notes in it. A well-used Bible is the greatest weapon against the power of the enemy.*

*Here are some things you have to know and do to use the Bible correctly.*

*Know that the Bible is completely true and is God's Word. 2 Peter 1:20-21 (ICB) says, "Most of all, you must understand this: No prophecy in the Scriptures ever comes from the prophet's own interpretation. No prophecy ever came from what a man wanted to say. But men led by the Holy Spirit spoke words from God." The Bible contains God's words. Even though lots of people wrote the books of the Bible, they didn't say what they wanted to say. They were led by the Holy Spirit and spoke the words of God.*

*There is also a lot of evidence that the Bible is true. Astronomers study the universe. A famous astronomer named Robert Jastrow said, "Now we see how the astronomical evidence leads to a biblical view of the origin of the world." (God and the Astronomers, Robert Jastrow, 2000)*

*Archeologists who dig up sites to study ancient civilizations have proven things in the Bible many times. But an archeologist has never found any digs that go against what the Bible says.*

*And there is more historical evidence about the Bible stories being true than evidence about famous people like Plato.*

*Besides that, the more we learn God's Word and the closer we get to God, the more we have faith that the Bible is God's Word.*

*God wants us to memorize Scripture, so we can think about it. In many places in the Bible, it tells us to meditate on God's Word. Memorizing Scripture helps us do that. If we know verses by heart, we can think about those verses even when we're not reading the Bible.*

Show tools. *If I didn't know how to use these tools, do you think I could fix anything?* Allow students to answer. *First, I'd need to learn how to use them the right way. Then I could fix things. It's the same with the Word of God. 2 Timothy 2:15 (NIV) says, "Do your best to present yourself to God as one approved, a worker who does not need to be ashamed and who correctly handles the word of truth." We need to study and learn the Word of God so we can be good workers who correctly use Scriptures.*

Show mirror. *How would it be if I looked in the mirror and saw my hair was messed up, but I didn't do anything about it? James 1:22 (NIV) says, "Do not merely listen to the word, and so deceive yourselves. Do what it says." If we study the Word of God but don't do what it says, we haven't grown up spiritually. Instead, we're like people who look in the mirror but don't do anything about their messed-up hair.*

*Sometimes kids and adults don't read the Bible because they don't understand it or they don't know how, but you have the Holy Spirit to help you understand God's Word. As we worship at the altar, let's ask the Holy Spirit to lead us and guide us in understanding the Bible.*

Have your students spend time worshipping. Lay hands on them and pray for them to have a greater desire for God's Word.

## Small Group Chat: Teach How to Study the Word of God

*Supplies needed:* Bible

In your own words, tell the students these facts about the Bible.

The Bible has 66 different books.

All of the books are about God and about Jesus even if Jesus isn't mentioned. Each book was written by an author. Some authors wrote many books. Some only wrote one.

The Bible has 2 parts. The Old Testament is about creation, the flood, and the people of Israel. It talks about the coming Messiah or Savior who will save the world from their sins. The New Testament tells about that Savior who is Jesus and about the early church. It also gives instruction for believers in Christ.

Different sections of the Bible:

The Law was about creation, early history, and the founding of Israel. It also listed the laws for Israel.

The Historical books are about the history of Israel before Jesus came.

The Poetry books have poetry about God in them.

The prophets, both major and minor, gave warnings from God and also told about the coming of Jesus.

The Gospels are about Jesus' life, death, and resurrection. Acts is the history of the early church.

Letter to the church were letters to the early church with instructions. Some letters were written by Paul. Some were written by others.

Revelation tells what's going to happen in the future.

Help students learn how to look up Scripture in their Bibles. Help them navigate YouVersion Kids or the Family Devotion Sheets.

# Lesson 12 – My Enemy

**Focus Point:** Demons are real, but we don't have to be afraid of them.

**Goal:** Students will learn that God is bigger than any demon, but there are doors they can open that invite demons into their lives.

**Verse of the Day: Ephesians 6:12 (NIV)** *For our struggle is not against flesh and blood, but against the rulers, against the authorities, against the powers of this dark world and against the spiritual forces of evil in the heavenly realms.*

**Supplies Needed:**

- *Building a Fortress in God* Downloadable Resources
- Kid James Puppet (optional)
- Army uniform costume for skit (optional)
- balloons
- classroom door
- rubber ears (optional)
- traffic light from lesson 3 (optional Make traffic light with theses supplies: cardboard or posterboard, glass, marker, red, yellow, and green tissue paper, scissor, tape or glue, flashlight)

**Opening**: *Building a Fortress in God Countdown* or *Building a Fortress in God* Slide (Available free with registration of this curriculum.)

**Welcome**: *Welcome to Building a Fortress in God. Today we're going to talk about something that isn't scary at all if you have given your life to Jesus. We're going to talk about demons. The reason they aren't scary is because demons are afraid of any Christian, no matter what age that Christian is, who has given his life to Jesus. Christ has power over every demon.*

**Prayer**: Ask a child to pray over the service. Encourage him or her to end the prayer with "In the Name of Jesus. Amen."

**Rules**: (use rules slide) Go over the 5 Ups Rules.

Go over the *5 Ups Rules*: 1. Sit up straight. 2. Listen up. 3. Hush up. 4. Don't get up and run around or go to the bathroom. 5. Worship Up! (stand up and participate during praise and worship)

**Theme or Activity Songs**: Choose one or two fast-moving activity or theme songs that go with the curriculum.

**Game Time: Balloon Wars** (use game time slide)

*Supplies Needed:* balloons

Divide students into teams of four to six players. The teams will get in a circle and hold hands. The teams will each get one balloon thrown into the center of their circle. They must keep the balloon in the air while holding hands. If a balloon touches the ground, or team members let go of each other's hands, or the balloon pops, that team is out. The team that keeps the balloon in the air the longest wins.

## Memory Verse Skit: (use *Building a Fortress in God* Lesson 12, slide a and/or Kid James Skit #12 Video)

*Supplies needed:* Kid James Puppet (optional)

*Kid James:* Howdy, kids. I'm Kid James. I'm a Bible, but not just any Bible. I teach children the Word of God. Today's verse is important to learn when it comes to spiritual warfare. Ephesians 6:12 (NIV) says, "For our struggle is not against flesh and blood, but against the rulers, against the authorities, against the powers of this dark world and against the spiritual forces of evil in the heavenly realms."

There is the physical world that we can also see, but there is also a spiritual world. We can't see it, but it is just as real as the physical world. Sometimes, when we struggle with things, it has nothing to do with us. Sometimes, spiritual forces of evil called demons are to blame. That's great news for a Christian because the Holy Spirit living on the inside of us is greater than any demon or even the devil himself.

## Offering:

*Sometimes, we struggle to give an offering to God because demonic forces try to convince us that we should keep our money. We don't have to listen to those demons. Everything we have is God's, so giving an offering is our way of showing God He is in charge of our lives.*

## Skit: Author's Testimony (use Testimony Skit #12 Video)

Sgt. Do Right will not appear today. Instead, show the students a video of the author's testimony, when she was involved in the occult as a child, and how Jesus set her free.

## Verse of the Day: Ephesians 6:12 (NIV) *For our struggle is not against flesh and blood, but against the rulers, against the authorities, against the powers of this dark world and against the spiritual forces of evil in the heavenly realms.*

## Memory Verse Talk: (use *Building a Fortress in God* Lesson 12, slide a)

Have your students repeat the verse a couple of times.

*Sometimes we think that our struggles and problems are with people, but that's not true according to today's memory verses. There is a war going on all the time between demons and angels that we can't even see. God sends angels to fight any powers that try to come against His children.*

## Memory Verse Activity: Act It Out (use *Building a Fortress in God* Lesson 12, slide a)

Divide students into teams. Give these teams five to ten minutes to come up with motions to act out today's memory verse. Allow the teams to act out the verse in front of the class.

## Bible Story: Disciples Confront the Occult

(Acts 16:16-18; Acts 19:13-19)

*Many times, when Jesus was on Earth, He cast demons out of people. If someone is a Christian, the Holy Spirit lives inside of him. He can also have power over demons in Jesus' name. Unless you are opening the door to demons through continuous sin, unforgiveness, or the occult, you don't have to be afraid of demons. They are afraid of you.*

*One time during the early church, Paul and Silas were preaching the Gospel in the streets of Thyatira. A slave girl was involved in fortune-telling and the occult. She had opened the door for a demon to come into her. She kept following Paul and Silas around, interrupting them and saying things like this: Listen to these men. They are servants of the most high God. What she said was true, but she was saying it in a way to distract people from what Paul and Silas were saying. She kept it up for days. In Acts 16:18 (NIV), "Finally Paul became so annoyed that he turned around and said to the spirit, 'In the name of Jesus Christ I command you to come out of her!' At that moment the spirit left her."*

*In another town, Paul and Silas were preaching, they prayed for many people who were healed and freed from demons. Seven men who were not Christians or followers of Jesus decided the name of Jesus was a magical name. They didn't realize that the reason we Christians pray in the name of Jesus is because we have the Holy Spirit in us to pray with the power of Jesus. They tried to use the name of Jesus whom Paul preached about to cast out demons. The demons attacked them in Acts 19:15 (NIV) saying, "I know Jesus, and I know Paul, but who are you?" Because of this many people were saved. A lot of them were into the occult, so they brought out their crystal balls, books, and other occult paraphernalia to Paul to destroy. The amount of occult things that were destroyed cost over one million dollars.*

*Maybe you've heard some of your friends or others say that you can pretend with the occult or use it for entertainment. It's just for fun. Don't believe it. The occult has the power of demons behind it. But the power of the Holy Spirit that lives inside of Christians is always more powerful than the power of any demon.*

**Praise and Worship:** Choose a couple of fast songs and a slow song to lead children into praise and worship. You can have a children's praise team, but until they understand leading praise and worship, have an adult leader or you be the worship leader.

## Object Lessons:

**1. Object Lesson: Opening Doors** (Use *Building a Fortress in God* Lesson 12, slides b-e)

*Supplies Needed:* Use the door in your room.

*Many years ago, the nation of Rome was greater and more powerful than any nation on Earth. It was a lot like the United States is today. It enjoyed many blessings like democracy and a good economy. The largest city in Rome was also called Rome. Many of the people of Rome had grown corrupt and sinful. They had wild parties and would get drunk a lot. Even the leaders and the army guarding the city were a part of those parties. When their enemies, the Germanic armies, invaded Rome, the army couldn't defend the city. The leaders opened the gates and gave the enemy all the riches hoping it would save their lives.*

Walk over to the door. Close it if it's not closed.

*Many fortresses in Bible times were strong enough to keep out any enemies, but every fortress has a door.* Open the door. *When you open the door, the enemy can come in.*

*That's true of our spiritual fortresses as well. God is more powerful than any demon or even the devil himself. Because the Holy Spirit is living inside of us, we can command any demon who tries to come against us to leave in Jesus' name, and he must obey. In the Bible story, you heard how Paul cast a demon out of a girl, and that demon had to leave. It is the same with us. God has built a fortress around us that no demon can get in.*

Close the door. *When we keep our spiritual doors closed, no weapon formed against us by demons can ever succeed. If you have bad dreams or night terrors, you can command that demon to leave your sleep alone, in the Name of Jesus, and he must obey. When a whole bunch of things go wrong or you're suddenly really confused about everything, it might be a demonic attack. You can tell that demon to leave you alone in Jesus' name, and again, he has to obey you. A Christian never has to be afraid of a demon unless…*

Open the door. *He opens the door. Of course, this isn't a physical door like this one. I'm talking about a spiritual door. A Christian can open a door when he allows sin to take over his life or when he refuses to forgive somebody. Another way a Christian opens the door to demons is when he is involved in the occult.*

Show slide b. *The occult is forbidden in the Bible and by God because it opens the door for demons to attack our lives. Deuteronomy 18:10-11 (NLT) says, "For example, never sacrifice your son or daughter as a burnt offering. And do not let your people practice fortune-telling, or use sorcery, or interpret omens, or engage in witchcraft, or cast spells, or function as mediums or psychics, or call forth the spirits of the dead."*

*To help you understand, I'll give you some examples of things that are part of the occult.*

Show slide c. *Sometimes you'll see signs or commercials advertising psychics who promise to help you by telling your future. While God sometimes sends prophets to speak to us about our future, we should never go to a psychic. A psychic is a fortune-teller like what is mentioned in the Bible. This opens the door to demons. But psychics aren't the only fortune-*

*tellers we need to avoid. Ouija boards, palm reading, astrology, 8-balls, tarot cards, and other devices all try to read our fortunes. They all open the door to the demonic.*

Show slide d. *Sorcery and witchcraft are also evil and open the door to demons. Sometimes people think there is good witchcraft called white magic and bad witchcraft called black magic. God doesn't make a distinction. He calls both evil. Witchcraft includes casting spells, moving objects with your mind, and transferring thoughts to other people. It also involves having spirit guides that are not the Holy Spirit. One example of having spirit guides is Pokemon. Each Pokemon character is a demonic Chinese spirit guide. Some kids think it's all right to watch movies or read books with witches in them or play Pokemon as long as they don't cast spells or have real spirit guides, but it's dangerous to allow any witchcraft into your lives.*

Show slide e. *Calling forth spirits of the dead is also occult and condemned by God. There are no such things as ghosts, but there are demons masquerading as ghosts. One of the things to avoid here is séances. Some kids think seances are harmless fun they do with their friends. But calling forth demons, disguised as ghosts, is not harmless.*

*There are other things that are occult as well. One way to avoid them is to ask for discernment.*

## 2. Object Lesson: Discernment of Spirits

*Supplies needed:* rubber ears (optional), traffic light from lesson 3 (optional. Make traffic light with these supplies: cardboard or posterboard, glass, marker, red, yellow, and green tissue paper, scissor, tape or glue, flashlight)

*Preparation:* To make a traffic light, cut a rectangle out of cardboard or posterboard. Draw three even circles by using the top of a glass to trace them. Cut red, yellow, and green squares of tissue paper large enough to cover the holes and attach them with tape or glue. Use a flashlight behind tissue paper to light up different colors.)

*In an earlier lesson, we learned how the Holy Spirit guides us. One way He guides us is through discernment of spirits. Discernment of spirits is a gift the Holy Spirit gives us, so we know if something is of God, or is demonic. Not everything that is not of God is demonic. Sometimes people sin because they want to, not because they were controlled by demons. But discernment helps us know that also.*

*Besides the Bible, the Holy Spirit will give us discernment by speaking to our spirit.* Show rubber ears or point to your ears. *We don't hear Him with our ears, at least most people don't. We hear Him right here.* Point to your stomach. *It's important to pray to the Holy Spirit for discernment.*

Show traffic light. *This traffic light will help you know what the Holy Spirit is telling you.*

Light up the red on the traffic light.

*Have you ever gone into a place or got near someone who made you feel yucky deep down inside? When that happens, it's important to listen to that feeling. That's the Holy Spirit letting you know something is wrong. It may not be demonic, but it might be.*

*Your friends might want to play a game that makes you feel yucky even though you don't know if that game is demonic. Or your teacher will want you to read a book you don't feel right about. Or you might be watching a television show or playing a video game that looks all right, and all of a sudden, you feel a red light in your spirit. It may be an adult who is a friend of your parents that makes you feel yucky. If that happens, explain to your parents how you feel and stay away from that person.*

*When you feel that yucky feeling in your stomach, stop what you're doing and listen to the Holy Spirit speaking to you.*

Light up the green light.

*You can be in a church service where strange things you've never seen before are happening. It might be the Holy Spirit, or it might not. Or your friend wants you to play a game you've never heard of before. You ask the Holy Spirit to give you discernment, and you don't feel that yucky feeling at all. Instead, you feel peace in your spirit. God is telling you everything is okay. You can go ahead.*

Light up the yellow light.

*Yellow means caution. Whatever you're doing, slow down. This happens when you are totally confused about whether something is okay or not. You don't have peace about it, but you don't feel that yucky feeling. When this happens, don't do anything. Instead, pray and ask God what He wants you to do. He will give you wisdom. If you still aren't sure, talk to that trusted adult and ask him or her to help you pray and decide.*

*As you listen for discernment, it will be easier for you to hear and know what to do. Adults who love God can help you with this if you're not sure.*

## Message: Closing Doors

*Jesus is greater, stronger, and more powerful than any demon or even Satan Himself.*

*The Holy Spirit who lives inside of Christians is greater, stronger, and more powerful than any demon or Satan himself. So we don't have to be afraid of demons.*

*Demons are controlled by Satan. At one time, they were angels, but they became evil. When Satan was an angel, he was called Lucifer. He was one of the most beautiful angels, but he rebelled against God. Most angels stayed loyal to God, but some followed Satan and became demons.*

*We know God, the Father, is more powerful than Satan because in the Bible, it says God cast*

*Satan and his demons out of Heaven.*

*We know Jesus Christ, the Son of God is more powerful than Satan because He had power over demons while He was on Earth. He also has power over Satan. Satan is even going to have to bow to Jesus and declare He is Lord. Philippians 2:9-11 (NIV) says, "Therefore God exalted him to the highest place and gave him the name that is above every name, that at the name of Jesus every knee should bow, in heaven and on earth and under the earth, and every tongue acknowledge that Jesus Christ is Lord, to the glory of God the Father."*

*We know that the Holy Spirit who lives inside of every Christian is more powerful than Satan. 1 John 4:4 (NIV) says, "You, dear children, are from God and have overcome them, because the one who is in you is greater than the one who is in the world."*

*All that means that if you have made Jesus your Lord and Savior, you don't have to be afraid of Satan or any of his demons unless you open the door.*

*Do you remember how you can open the door?* Allow students to answer.

*You can open a door by getting involved in sin. If you've done that, you can ask Jesus to forgive you and help you not to sin that way again and close that door.*

*Unforgiveness opens a door. If you are angry at someone and haven't forgiven that person, ask Jesus to forgive you. Pray for the person you are angry with and ask God to help you forgive him. Do that, and you will close that door.*

*The occult opens a door. If you have been involved in the occult in any way, ask Jesus to forgive you and declare that every demonic force you've let in has to leave in the name of Jesus. If you have any occult materials, you need to get rid of them. You can throw them away, or you can bring them to me next week, and I'll destroy them, but you need to get them out of your house. If your parents or siblings have occult materials, you don't have to be afraid. The Holy Spirit in you is greater than any demon. Get rid of the occult in your life, and you will close that door.* Slam shut the door of your classroom.

*James 4:7 (NIV) says, "Submit yourselves, then, to God. Resist the devil, and he will flee from you."*

*We are going to spend the next few minutes submitting ourselves to God in worship. If you have anything to ask God for forgiveness, you can do it now. If you've not forgiven someone, pray for that person now and ask God to help you forgive. If you've been involved in the occult, ask God to forgive you and declare that you are getting rid of the occult in your life.*

For response time, spend some time in worship. After the worship is done, lead your students in a prayer dedicating yourselves to God and resisting the devil in every way.

## Small Group Chat: Occult Checklist

*Talk to students about what things might be included in the occult and what things they might want to stop doing or get rid of.*

# Lesson 13 – Our Victory

**Focus Point:** Because God is my refuge, I don't need to be afraid

**Goal:** Students will learn that God is on their side, so they don't have to worry or fear any danger.

**Verse of the Day: Revelation 12:11a (NIV)** *They triumphed over him by the blood of the Lamb and by the word of their testimony.*

**Supplies Needed:**

- *Building a Fortress in God* Downloadable Resources
- Kid James Puppet (optional)
- Army uniform costume for skit (optional)
- three crowns (Burger King crowns or construction paper crowns)
- basketball
- 2 clear glasses
- Water
- dissolvo paper (You can purchase dissolvo paper online or at a local magic shop.)
- marker
- red food coloring
- bean bag
- tug-of-war rope
- 3 sets of gloves to protect hands
- party decorations
- cupcakes or cookies
- drinks
- ice cream

**Opening:** *Building a Fortress in God Countdown* or *Building a Fortress in God* Slide (Available free with registration of this curriculum.)

**Welcome:** *Welcome to Building a Fortress in God. God is mighty, mightier than anything in the universe. He created the universe. He also loves His children, those who have accepted Him as their Savior. So if you are a child of God, there is never any reason to be afraid. That doesn't mean you won't feel the emotion of fear. That's normal. But it does mean you can trust God to be a present help in time of trouble. God is mightier than anything you fear.*

**Prayer:** Ask a child to pray over the service. Encourage him or her to end the prayer with "In the Name of Jesus. Amen."

**Rules:** (use rules slide) Go over the 5 Ups Rules.

Go over the *5 Ups Rules*: 1. Sit up straight. 2. Listen up. 3. Hush up. 4. Don't get up and run around or go to the bathroom. 5. Worship Up! (stand up and participate during praise and worship)

**Theme or Activity Songs:** Choose one or two fast-moving activity or theme songs that go with the curriculum.

## Game Time: Crown Him (use game time slide)

*Supplies Needed:* three crowns (Burger King crowns or construction paper crowns)

*In the Bible, it says that Jesus is King of Kings and Lord of Lord. It also says in the book of Revelation, the last book in the Bible, that we will be rewarded with crowns by God, but we will give them all to Jesus.*

Choose one student to be king. The other students will take turns trying to throw three crowns onto the king's head. You can do as many rounds as you like. If any students throw all three crowns on the king's head, they win.

## Memory Verse Skit: (use *Building a Fortress in God* Lesson 13, slide a and/or Kid James Skit #13 Video)

*Supplies needed:* Kid James Puppet (optional)

*Kid James:* Howdy, kids. I'm Kid James. I'm a Bible, but not just any Bible. I teach children the Word of God. Today's verse is in Revelation 12:11a (NIV) It says, "They triumphed over him by the blood of the Lamb and by the word of their testimony." Triumph is a big word for winning a victory in a battle or in sports. Jesus won the victory over Satan when He died on the cross and shed His blood for us and rose again on the third day. If we have accepted Christ's sacrifice of His blood and given our lives to Jesus Christ, we are children of God. Jesus' triumph is our triumph. We can plead Christ's blood whenever we are attacked, but there's something more we can do. We can declare that victory by talking about what Jesus has done for us. When we do that, we are giving our testimony. Because Jesus is victorious, we are victorious.

## Offering:

*One way we can be victorious in Christ is to give an offering. When we give an offering, we are showing the devil that we belong to God because even our money belongs to God.*

## Skit: Sgt. Do Right and the Victory (use Sgt. Do Right Skit #13 Video)

*Supplies Needed:* Army uniform (optional)

(Sgt. Do Right marches into the room and salutes.)

*Leader:* Hello, Sgt. Do Right.

*Sgt. Do Right:* Sgt. Do Right reporting as ordered, Sir (Ma'am).

*Leader:* I'm so glad you're here for our last lesson in *Building a Fortress in God.*

*Sgt. Do Right:* Thank you, Sir (Ma'am). I wouldn't want to miss it. God has really helped me in these lessons. I learned that because I'm a child of God, God gives me armor, and He gives me the authority of His name. In every way, He protects me. I don't have to be afraid.

*Leader:* That's right Sgt. Do Right. Do you know what you just did?

*Sgt. Do Right:* What did I do?

*Leader:* You gave your testimony.

*Sgt. Do Right:* My testimony?

*Leader:* You just told us what God has done for you. That's called a testimony. Our Scripture for today in Revelation 12:11a (NIV) says, "They triumphed over him by the blood of the Lamb and by the word of their testimony." When you told us what God has done for you, you gave us the word of your testimony.

*Sgt. Do Right:* That's awesome, but what about the other part?

*Leader:* What other part?

*Sgt. Do Right:* The blood of the Lamb thing. How do I get that? Do I need to find some shepherd somewhere and buy a lamb?

*Leader:* No, of course not. Jesus is called the Lamb of God who shed His blood for our sins. If we have given our lives to Him, we can plead His blood over our circumstances. He has already won the victory with His blood that He shed for our sins.

*Sgt. Do Right:* I need to tell everyone about this. This is such great news. Bye.

(Salutes and exits)

**Verse of the Day: Revelation 12:11a (NIV)** *They triumphed over him by the blood of the Lamb and by the word of their testimony.*

**Memory Verse Talk:** (use *Building a Fortress in God* Lesson 13, slide a)

Have your students repeat the verse a couple of times.

*According to this verse, if you have given your life to Jesus, you have already won the victory over the devil because of Jesus' blood. If trouble comes your way, you can plead the blood. What that means is you tell that trouble that Jesus shed His blood for you so you have the victory.*

*The second part of the verse is important too. We need to remember what God has done for us. Sometimes, it's easy to forget when something bad happens that Jesus saved us from our sins, and because of Him, we will spend eternity in Heaven. When we remind ourselves and other people by speaking the words about what Jesus has done for us, we win the victory over our sadness and discouragement.*

### Memory Verse Activity: Bounce the Word (use *Building a Fortress in God* Lesson 13, slide a)

*Supplies needed:* basketball

Have the students stand in a circle. Instruct them that each time they catch the ball, they have to say the next word of the verse, then bounce the ball to another student. Start it off by saying the address of the verse and bouncing the ball to a student.

### Bible Story: Jesus Won the Victory Over Satan (use *Building a Fortress in God* Lesson 13, slide b)

(Revelation 19:11-20)

*When Jesus died on the cross, He shed His blood so we could have a relationship with God. Then, on the third day, He defeated Satan completely and rose from the dead.*

*Colossians 2:15 (NIV) says, "And having disarmed the powers and authorities, he made a public spectacle of them, triumphing over them by the cross."*

*When armies won in Bible days, they would take their enemy's weapons and have a parade showing everyone they won. That's what Jesus did when He died on the cross and rose from the dead. He took Satan's weapons from him and had a parade in Heaven making a spectacle of the devil and his demons. Because of what Jesus did, when we give our lives to Him, we have victory over Satan.*

*But there's another battle Jesus is going to fight with Satan someday. It's called the Battle of Armageddon.*

*During the battle of Armageddon, Satan is going to use evil armies of this world to try to destroy Christians one last time.*

Show slide b. *Jesus is going to ride in on a white horse wearing a white robe dipped in the blood from the cross. His eyes will blaze like fire, and He'll have the Sword of the Spirit coming out of His mouth. He'll have many crowns on His head, and He'll wear a sash with the name, "King of Kings, and Lord of Lords." It won't be a scary time for us Christians, but it will be a very scary time for Satan and his demons.*

*All of us Christians will get to be in the Lord's army. We'll wear white robes and ride white horses, and we'll ride behind Jesus Christ as He defeats Satan and his demons. Satan and his demons will be thrown in the lake of fire called Hades for a thousand years, and we'll never have to worry about him again.*

*I'm sure glad I'm on God's side and that Jesus Christ is my King and my Lord.*

**Praise and Worship:** Choose a couple of fast songs and a slow song to lead children into praise and worship. Today would be a good day for a song about the blood of Jesus. You can have a children's praise team, but until they understand leading praise and worship, have an adult leader or you be the worship leader.

## Object Lessons:

### 1. Object Lesson: Pleading the Blood

*Supplies Needed:* 2 clear glasses, water, dissolvo paper (You can purchase dissolvo paper online or at a local magic shop.), marker, red food coloring

*Preparation:* Fill the first glass with water. Place 2-3 drops of red food coloring in the bottom of the second glass. Write problems on the piece of dissolvo paper with the marker.

*When we give our lives to Jesus, the blood Jesus shed on the cross cleanses us from our sins, from every bad thing we've ever done. Because of Jesus' blood we are saved and become children of God.*

*But have you ever noticed that Christians still have problems? That's normal. But we can plead the blood of Jesus over those problems, and God will be with us to win the victory over them.*

Pick up the second glass so that you cover up the food coloring. *How many of you have problems whether at school, or at home, or maybe with your friends?* Allow students to answer. Choose one student you know is saved.

*Do you see that piece of paper on the table? Pick it up and read it.* If the student has difficulty reading, tell the student what the paper says. *I want you to take that paper and fold it three times until it's small.* Have the students do so. *Now stick the paper into this empty glass.* Have the student do so.

*Many Christians know the blood of Jesus saves them and cleanses them from their sins. But the blood of Jesus in a Christian's life does much more. If we sin after we are saved, the blood of Jesus cleanses us from that sin. It redeems us, which means, not only does God forgive us, but He helps us to avoid that sin in the future.*

*The blood of Jesus also delivers us. When we're facing an attack of the enemy, or some battle or problem, or we need healing in our bodies, the blood of Jesus will deliver us.*

*The blood of Jesus also protects us. During the time of Moses, in the Old Testament, God sent a plague to deliver the Jewish people from their oppressors. The Jewish people painted*

*lamb's blood over their doors, and everyone inside, even if they weren't Jewish, were protected. The Lamb of God is Jesus Christ. The blood He shed for us on the cross is our protection. When we accept Jesus into our lives, we have the right to plead the blood of Jesus to protect us.*

Have the student repeat the following. *I am a child of God. I plead the blood over my problems.* Pour the water in the first glass into the second glass. The water will turn red. Continue to pour the water from glass to glass until the paper is dissolved. Then ask the student to pull out the paper. When the student remarks that the paper is gone, say that the blood of Jesus dissolves our problems.

**2. Object Lesson: The Word of Our Testimony**

*Supplies needed:* bean bag

Find one or two people in your church who are willing to give a short testimony at this time.

*We not only defeat Satan and his demons by the blood Jesus shed on the cross. We also defeat him by the word of our testimony. I asked a couple of adults in our church to give testimonies of what God has done in their lives.*

Have the adults give testimonies. Explain that the beanbag you have in your hand is a testimony bean bag. When you throw it to a student, that student has to give a testimony of what God has done in his life. Make sure everyone has a turn, then throw the bean bag in the air, catch it, and give your testimony.

*When we are going through troubles, it helps if we remember what God has done for us and hear what God has done for others. Testimony time is one way we defeat the enemy.*

## Message: We are Victorious Because Jesus Goes Before Us

*Supplies Needed:* tug-of-war rope, 3 sets of gloves to protect hands

For this message, you will need a strong teenager or full-grown man. Choose the smallest student in your class and the largest student in your class. Make sure ahead of time that the second student knows he's representing Satan and that he's all right with that. Have them each hold opposite ends of the rope.

*We're going to have a tug-of-war contest. Which one do you think will win?* Hold your hand over each participant, and have the students cheer for the one they think will win. They will most likely choose the larger student.

*But wait.* Point to the smallest participant. *This student is a child of God. The blood of Jesus has cleansed her and protects her. She has an armor of light around her. She knows the Name of Jesus is her fortress and she trusts the Holy Spirit to guide her. The joy of the Lord is her strength, and her worship is a weapon. She's fitted with the armor of God, including the belt of truth, the breastplate of righteousness, the helmet of salvation, and the shoes of the Gospel of Peace. She holds the shield of faith in one hand and the sword of the Spirit, the Word of God, in the other. She doesn't open doors to the enemy, and she loves to tell what Jesus has done in her life.*

Point to the other student. *And this student represents Satan. Does anyone want to change their mind about who's going to win?* Allow students to answer.

*Let the contest begin.* Immediately the man steps in and stops it. *Wait. I'm Jesus Christ, and this is my child. I fight her battles for her.* He grabs the rope on the smallest student's side and stands with the students. *Now let the battle begin.* Tug-of-war contest begins, and of course, the side with Jesus wins.

*And* (name of the smallest child) *is the winner and the champion. When we've asked Jesus into our hearts and lives, He applies the blood of the Lamb to our lives. We have everything we need to fight and win the victory against the enemy because Jesus Christ fights our battles for us. Now that is a testimony.*

For response time, lead students into a prayer of victory. Ask if anyone is fighting a battle right now. Anoint and pray for them. During worship time, worship to a victory song.

## Celebration Time

*Supplies needed:* party decorations, cupcakes or cookies, drinks, ice cream

*When a sports team wins a victory, they have a party to celebrate, so we are going to end this series with a party.*

Have a celebration party with your students.

# Meet the Author

Pastor Tamera Kraft has been a children's pastor for over thirty years. She is the director of a ministry called Revival Fire For Kids, where she mentors other children's leaders, teaches workshops, and is a children's ministry consultant and children's revivalist. She is a recipient of the 2007 National Children's Leaders Association Shepherd's Cup for lifetime achievement in children's ministry.

Tamera hosts a children's ministry podcast called IGNITE KIDMIN, available on most podcast providers and provides coaching and resources for IGNITE KIDMIN patron subscribers. Find out more about this at http://revivalfire4kids.com/ignite.

You can find out more about Revival Fire for Kids at http://revivalfire4kids.com.